Com~~puter Installation~~ and Acceptance

IT Infrastructure Library

John Coles

Gildengate House,
Upper Green Lane,
NORWICH, NR3 1DW

London: HMSO

004 RT

© Crown Copyright 1993

Applications for reproduction
should be made to HMSO

First published   1993
ISBN   0 11 330556 7
ISSN   0956-2591

This is one of the books in the IT Infrastructure Library series. At regular intervals, further books will be published and the Library will be completed in 1993. Since many customers would like to receive the IT Infrastructure Library books automatically on publication, a standing order service has been set up. For further details on standing orders please contact:

HMSO Publicity (PU23 E3), FREEPOST,
Norwich, NR3 1BR
(*No stamp needed for UK customers*).

Until the whole Library is published, and subject to availability, draft copies of unpublished books may be obtained from CCTA if you are a standing order customer. To obtain drafts please contact:

IT Infrastructure Management Services
CCTA
Gildengate House, Upper Green Lane,
NORWICH, NR3 1DW.

For further information on other CCTA products, contact:

Press and Publications,
Room 3/9
CCTA
Gildengate House,
Upper Green Lane,
NORWICH, NR3 1DW.

This document has been produced using procedures conforming to
BS 5750 Part 1: 1987; ISO 9001: 1987.

Table of contents

1.	**Management summary**	**1**
2.	**Introduction**	**3**
2.1	Purpose	3
2.2	Target readership	4
2.3	Scope	4
2.4	Related guidance	6
2.5	Standards	8
3.	**Planning for Computer Installation and Acceptance**	**9**
3.1	Procedures	9
3.1.1	Preparing accommodation on a greenfield site	10
3.1.2	Planning to install computer equipment in an existing or new environment	17
3.2	Dependencies	32
3.2.1	Project funding	32
3.2.2	Project management tools and techniques	33
3.2.3	Configuration and Change Management	33
3.2.4	Problem Management	34
3.2.5	Acceptance plans	34
3.3	People	34
3.3.1	IT Services Manager	34
3.3.2	Project Board	35
3.3.3	Project Manager	35
3.3.4	Project team	36
3.3.5	Suppliers	36
3.3.6	Support staff	37
3.3.7	Others involved	37
3.3.8	Recruitment	38
3.3.9	Training	39
3.3.10	Overtime and extended hours during acceptance	40
3.4	Timing	40
3.4.1	Project duration	40
3.4.2	Equipment lead times	40
3.4.3	Staff training	41

IT Infrastructure Library
Computer Installation and Acceptance

4.	Implementation	43
4.1	Procedures	43
4.1.1	Receiving new equipment and software	44
4.1.2	Installation of new hardware	44
4.1.3	Installation of new software	46
4.1.4	Acceptance testing	46
4.1.5	Associated disciplines	48
4.1.6	Equipment handover	50
4.1.7	Security	51
4.1.8	Health and Safety	51
4.2	Dependencies	51
4.3	People	52
4.3.1	Operations staff	52
4.3.2	Systems Programmers	52
4.3.3	Hardware support	52
4.4	Timing	52

5.	Post-implementation and audit	55
5.1	Procedures	55
5.1.1	Project evaluation review	55
5.1.2	Post-implementation review	56
5.1.3	Ongoing management	56
5.1.4	Further installations	57
5.2	Dependencies	57
5.3	People	57
5.4	Timing	57

6.	Benefits, costs and possible problems	59
6.1	Benefits	59
6.2	Costs	59
6.3	Possible problems	60
6.3.1	Resistance to change	60
6.3.2	Project Management	61
6.3.3	Accommodation handover and equipment delivery	61
6.3.4	Integration of multi-vendor equipment	61
6.3.5	User expectations	61

7.	**Tools**	**63**
7.1	Introduction	63
7.2	Types of tool	63
7.2.1	Project Management	63
7.2.2	Security risk analysis	64
7.2.3	Design and modelling	64
7.2.4	Configuration Management	65
7.2.5	Spreadsheet	65
7.2.6	Word Processing	65
8.	**Bibliography**	**67**

Annexes

A.	**Glossary of terms**	**A1**
B.	**Acceptance procedures**	**B1**
B.1	Preparation for and performance of acceptance procedures	B1
B.1.1	Preparation for acceptance procedures	B2
B.1.2	Performance of acceptance procedures	B2
B.1.3	Downtime	B3
B.1.4	Calculation of serviceability	B3
B.2	Acceptance procedures and acceptance criteria	B4
B.2.1	Conditions for acceptance	B4
B.2.2	Acceptance procedures	B4
C.	**Procurement guidance**	**C1**
D.	**Standards**	**D1**
D.1	Introduction	D1
D.2	Computer room sizes	D1
D.3	Electrical and mechanical design standards	D1
D.3.1	General	D1
D.3.2	Safety	D1
D.3.3	Equipment	D2
D.3.4	Installation	D2
D.4	Fire protection and life safety systems	D2
D.4.1	General	D2
D.4.2	Safety	D2

IT Infrastructure Library
Computer Installation and Acceptance

E.	**Installation procedures**	**E1**
E.1	Hardware	E1
E.2	System and applications software	E2

Foreword

Welcome to the IT Infrastructure Library module on **Computer Installation and Acceptance.**

In their respective areas the IT Infrastructure Library publications complement and provide more detail than the IS Guides.

The ethos behind the development of the IT Infrastructure Library is the recognition that organizations are becoming increasingly dependent on IT in order to satisfy their corporate aims and meet their business needs. This growing dependency leads to growing requirement for quality IT services. In this context quality means 'matched to business needs and user requirements as these evolve'.

This module is one of a series of codes of practice intended to facilitate the quality management of IT services and of the IT Infrastructure. (By IT Infrastructure, we mean organizations' computers and networks - hardware, software and computer related communications, upon which application systems and IT services are built and run). The codes of practice will assist organizations to provide quality IT services in the face of skill shortages, system complexity, rapid change, growing user expectations, current and future user requirements.

Underpinning the IT Infrastructure is the Environmental Infrastructure upon which it is built. Environmental topics are covered in separate sets of guides within the IT Infrastructure Library.

IT infrastructure management is a complex subject which for presentational and practical reasons has been broken down within the IT Infrastructure Library into a series of modules. A complete list of current and planned modules is available from the CCTA IT Infrastructure Management Services at the address given at the back of this module.

The structure of the module is, in essence:

* a **Management summary** aimed at senior managers (Directors of IT and above, typically down to Civil Service Grade 5), senior IT staff and, in some cases, users or office managers (typically Civil Service Grades 5 to 7)

* the main body of the text, aimed at IT middle management (typically grades 7 to HEO)

* technical detail in Annexes.

IT Infrastructure Library
Computer Installation and Acceptance

The module gives the main **guidance** in sections 3 to 5; explains the **benefits, costs and possible problems** in section 6, which may be of interest to senior staff; and provides information on **tools** (requirements and examples of real-life availability) in section 7.

CCTA is working with the IT industry to foster the development of software tools to underpin the guidance contained within the codes of practice (ie to make adherence to the module more practicable), and ultimately to automate functions.

If you have any comments on this or other modules, do please let us know. A **Comments sheet** is provided with every module. Alternatively you may wish to contact us directly using the reference point given in **Further information**.

Thank you. We hope you find this module useful.

Acknowledgement

The assistance of the following contributors is gratefully acknowledged:

Bryan James (under contract to CCTA from IBM United Kingdom Ltd)

Henry Harris (under contract to CCTA from The ISIS Partnership).

1. Management summary

Background
: Computers are now at the core of successful operation of most organizations. Whether they are successfully integrated within the organization depends on the answers to such questions as:

  * do they satisfy a business need?
  * was the timing of their introduction sensible?
  * do they enable data to be made available at the right place and at the right time?
  * do they provide new ways of solving problems, that could not be tackled using other approaches?
  * are they easy to use?

This module
: This module provides guidance on the installation and acceptance of large scale computer equipment for integration into an IT infrastructure (hardware, software and telecommunications). By *large scale computer equipment* we mean computers such as mainframes which require a controlled environment. The module does not cover the installation of distributed processing (wide area networks, local area networks and servers), local processors and terminals or telecommunications networks. These topics are covered by other modules in the Library.

  It also addresses greenfield sites, covering the management of site planning, the preparation of computer accommodation, supplier supervision during installation, inventory control of assets, acceptance testing, parallel running, and all forms of IT system upgrade.

The project approach
: Large scale computers are complex and their introduction into an IT infrastructure will require skilled staff of many disciplines to be brought together. These disciplines have a high degree of interdependence and involve people from within and outside the organization.

  In this module, the installation of computer equipment is regarded as a complex project, requiring forethought, planning, assessment of risks, and expertise, especially in project management. The timely availability of IT services to the users will be dependent on the quality of this planning activity.

The IT Infrastructure Library
Computer Installation and Acceptance

Benefits　　　　　　　　　　The aim of this module is to indicate the importance of effective management during the planning and installation of new equipment and software. The key benefits to be gained are minimal disruption to the business operation, fewer teething problems and increased user satisfaction.

Section 2
Introduction

2. Introduction

In 1987, the Butler Cox Foundation surveyed its members on the subject of data centre planning. The main issues identified at that time were:

* the likely trends in the performance and space requirements for data-storage devices and processors
* the impact of distributed computing on the corporate data centre
* the trend towards unmanned data centres
* the security measures that could be taken to protect the data centre premises and the equipment and data housed in them.

Today some of these trends are more predictable and, no doubt, if the survey were repeated, other concerns would be voiced. It is clear that Information Technology(IT) is still developing at enormous speed and that development shows no sign of slowing down. Computer accommodation, on the other hand, takes a long time to plan and build and will outlive many generations of computer hardware. It can be much more difficult to adapt a building to changing needs than to change a computer system. Therefore computer accommodation must be carefully planned, taking into account future expansion whilst having the flexibility to absorb unforeseen circumstances.

Despite the trend towards downsizing and distributed computing, there is still a requirement for large centralized computer centres. The primary focus of this module is to provide guidance on the installation and acceptance of larger computers. However much of the guidance is relevant to installations of all sizes.

2.1 Purpose

The purpose of this module is to assist organizations to ensure that, in installing new computers, they:

* meet budgets and timescales
* satisfy IT requirements in relation to business needs
* avoid disrupting existing IT services
* protect IT assets
* protect the organization's rights in the event of conflict with suppliers

* avoid the nugatory costs of poorly managed projects
* avoid or reduce the risk of failure.

The above objectives are particularly relevant when installing computer equipment of high value (where there is much to lose), or where there is a high risk of disrupting the business operation. The guidance on planning, installing equipment, and acceptance testing contained in sections 3.1 and 4.1 of this module will help organizations achieve these objectives.

2.2 Target readership

The information presented in the module is aimed at IT Services Managers, Computer Operations Managers and those members of project boards and project teams involved with overseeing the installation and testing of computer equipment. The module will also be of interest to people responsible for providing computer accommodation and to people responsible for buying computers.

2.3 Scope

The module gives guidance to organizations on planning for and managing the installation and acceptance of large scale computer equipment for integration into an IT infrastructure.

Figure 1, opposite, shows the scope of the module including the relationships between computer accommodation, the procurement cycle, equipment and documentation. The module relates specifically to the installation of large IT equipment which requires a controlled environment. The installation of smaller equipment is covered by the module on **Management of Local Processors and Terminals** and the installation of networks is covered in **Network Management**.

This module covers the management aspects of computer installation and acceptance, including:

* site planning
* preparation of computer accommodation
* relationships with suppliers during installation and the immediate post-implementation period
* inventory control of assets
* acceptance testing of hardware and software as delivered

Section 2
Introduction

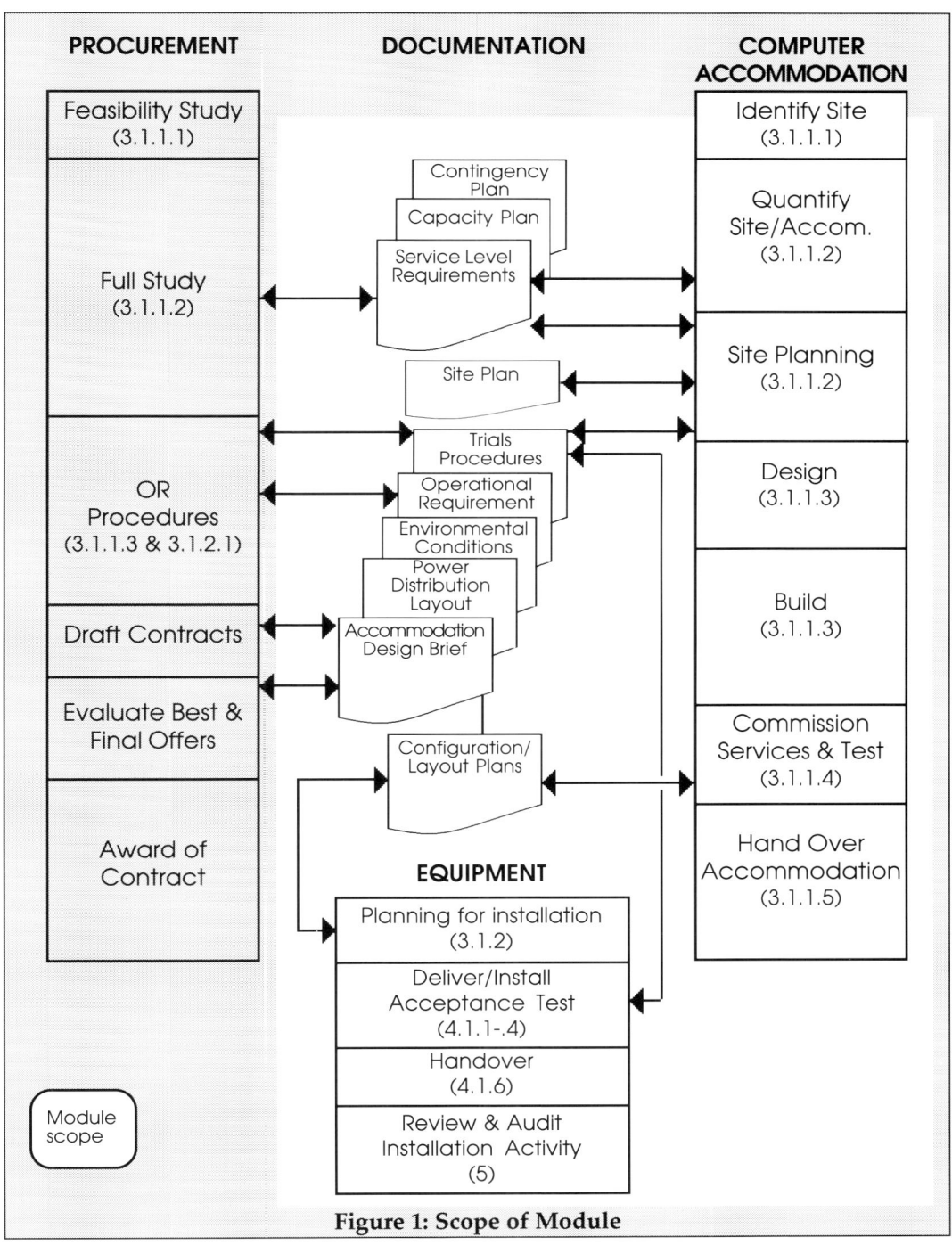

Figure 1: Scope of Module

* parallel running
* upgrades.

The module does not address the technical aspects of these topics in any detail as they are either installation and hardware specific or are covered by other modules in the IT Infrastructure Library. For instance, the technical specification of computer accommodation requirements is covered in the **Accommodation Specification** module in the Environmental Management set. Here we refer to the need for an Accommodation Design Brief and describe how it is used in the planning process.

This module makes the following assumptions:

* the decision to buy large central computers has already been made
* funding for the purchase of new equipment has been planned and authorized
* development of new or bespoke software to run on the new equipment is a separate project
* a procurement project to purchase the new equipment is already under way.

2.4 Related guidance

This book is one of a series of modules issued as part of the CCTA IT Infrastructure Library. Although the module can be read in isolation, it should be used in conjunction with other modules:

* **Accommodation Specification** - provides guidance on the technical aspects of preparing a specification for a new computer centre.
* **Availability Management** - provides guidance on specifying equipment requirements for the availability of IT services. It also contains guidance on serviceability monitoring which can be applied to monitoring acceptance trials as well as normal day-to-day operation.
* **Cable Infrastructure Strategy** - strategic cabling issues are considered, along with the costs and benefits of planning, installing and maintaining a cable infrastructure.
* **Capacity Management** - provides guidance on predicting equipment requirements to meet the

performance criteria specified in Service Level Agreements, and on performance monitoring, for example during acceptance trials.

* **Change Management** - includes guidance on major changes such as building computer accommodation and installing IT equipment. These activities must be properly managed.

* **Configuration Management** - all equipment (hardware, software and communications) on order, installed, under test or in use, and any status changes thereto, must be recorded in the Configuration Management Database. This module describes Configuration Management in an IT environment.

* **Contingency Planning** - describes how resilience requirements have a considerable influence on site and configuration planning. For example, it may be desirable to spread computing power over two or more networked sites to provide resilience to a major failure at one site.

* **Environmental Standards for Equipment Accommodation** - provides details of the standards to be applied when specifying computer accommodation to designers and suppliers.

* **Fire Precautions in IT Installations** - looks at the principal aspects of fire precautions in both dedicated computer accommodation and offices containing IT equipment

* **Managing Supplier Relationships** - describes the management of relationships with the suppliers and maintainers of hardware, software and network equipment.

* **Network Management** - covers the installation and acceptance of networks.

* **Service Level Management** - refers to the need for sufficient equipment to be installed to enable service level requirements to be met in respect of availability and performance.

* **Specification and Management of a Cable Infrastructure** - a practical guide to planning, specifying and managing a cable infrastructure installation project.

Other books which are referenced in this module are listed in section 8, Bibliography.

2.5 Standards

BS7083 - Recommendations for the accommodation and operating environment of computer equipment. British Standards Institution - 1989

ISO9001/EN29000/BS5750 - Quality Management and Quality Assurance Standards.

The IT Infrastructure Library modules are being designed to assist adherents to obtain third-party quality certification to ISO9001. Organizations' IT Directorates may wish to be so certified and CCTA will in future recommend that Facilities Management providers are also certified, by a third party certification body, to ISO9000. Such third parties should be accredited by NACCB, the National Accreditation Council for Certification Bodies.

Further information on related and important standards is contained in Annex D.

3. Planning for Computer Installation and Acceptance

This section contains guidance on planning and managing site preparation. It also covers the planning for the installation of equipment, into either a greenfield site or existing accommodation. These activities should be managed as a project and carried out by a project team. Indeed the size of the project may well necessitate the formation of several sub-projects, especially if there is new building work and new computer equipment to be procured. However, it is important that all sub-projects should be co-ordinated by a single project manager.

Reference should be made to Figure 1 (page 5), which describes the relationships between the activities of:

* building computer accommodation
* the procurement process
* equipment planning, installation and handover

and the supporting documentation.

3.1 Procedures

The project should be managed using a recognized method, with sign-off procedures at every stage. The preferred government method for project management is PRINCE (PRojects IN Controlled Environments).

Project Manager — The first task is to select a Project Manager, who should be appointed by the Project Board. Further information on the qualities required by a Project Manager is contained in section 3.3.3. It should be noted that he or she has a pivotal role and that selection of the right person is crucial to the success of the project.

Route map — The remainder of section 3.1 has been divided into two sub-sections. Sub-section 3.1.1 gives guidance on planning to build new computer accommodation, whilst 3.1.2 deals with planning to install equipment into previously prepared accommodation. Hence, those readers who are faced with a greenfield site should read 3.1.1 and 3.1.2 whilst those who already have some suitable computer accommodation may proceed directly to 3.1.2.

The IT Infrastructure Library
Computer Installation and Acceptance

3.1.1 Preparing accommodation on a greenfield site

This section deals with:

* identifying a site
* quantifying computer accommodation requirements
* designing and building the accommodation
* commissioning and testing the accommodation
* handover of the computer accommodation.

3.1.1.1 Identifying a site

Selecting the location of the site is outside the scope of this module, but if a site has not already been identified, it should be considered during the Feasibility Study. The Corporate Business Plan and the IS Strategy should be examined for factors that may influence the choice of site. Some of the key items that need consideration are listed below:

* availability and cost of land
* building costs
* staffing costs
* availability of suitable staff
* availability of maintenance facilities
* contingency/disaster recovery requirements
* resilience requirements
* access to electrical power of sufficient capacity and reliability
* access to communications facilities
* proximity to high levels of electromagnetic radiation, such as large RADAR installations
* possible hazards, eg flooding
* security requirements
* proximity to users and customers.

A CCTA Risk Analysis and Management Method (CRAMM) review should be conducted at a high level to determine the outline security requirements and physical security measures to be included in the new accommodation. This review will identify the assets and potential threats, vulnerabilities and countermeasures.

At the end of the Feasibility Study, a report should be published containing costed options and recommendations for the way ahead, project plans and resource plans for the next stage, the Full Study. Feasibility and Full Studies are described in the 'B Set' of IS Guides, produced by CCTA.

3.1.1.2 Quantifying computer accommodation requirements

During the Full Study, more detail will be required on the type and amount of accommodation to be built and its layout. A further, more detailed, CRAMM review should be carried out. This review will consider the assets in greater detail and refine the threats, vulnerabilities and countermeasures previously identified.

The specification of both the equipment and the computer accommodation (including plant rooms) will require input from Service Level Agreements (existing services) or Service Level Requirements (future service needs), Capacity Plans and Contingency Plans.

Service Level Agreements provide information on the performance and availability requirements for the IT services under normal and emergency conditions. The capacity planning process takes these requirements and calculates computing needs, data storage and data communications capacity required for the future.

A Capacity Plan should be produced which presents these calculations for management consideration. (Further information on capacity planning and computer sizing is contained in the IT Infrastructure Library module on **Capacity Management**.) From this sizing the requirements for the computer accommodation (eg space, cooling, trunking) can be estimated and a start made on layout planning.

Following on from the CRAMM review, a Contingency Plan should be produced. This will be used to specify the computer accommodation requirements for disaster recovery purposes. For instance, this may mean splitting the computer accommodation over two separate buildings or sites in order to reduce vulnerability.

The IT Infrastructure Library
Computer Installation and Acceptance

If existing applications are to be transferred to computers in the new accommodation, these Service Level Agreements, Capacity Plans and Contingency Plans should exist already, or at least there should be a body of knowledge which will enable them to be produced. If applications development is taking place in parallel with the computer accommodation project, it should be possible to obtain a degree of requirements information, depending on the stage of development. This sizing information will become progressively more accurate as the new applications are developed. Further information on this topic is contained in the CCTA ISE Library publication **SSADM and Capacity Planning**.

Plans should be made at this stage to manage the installation and acceptance of equipment into the new accommodation (please refer to 3.1.2.6 and 3.1.2.7 for further information on planning the installation and acceptance of equipment into new or existing accommodation).

The implementation policy should be decided, since this may affect the space and power requirements. For instance, if there is a need to continue running existing applications, are these to be transferred to the new site? Will this require the existing equipment to be housed alongside the incoming new equipment on a temporary or semi-permanent basis? If so, then the space requirements must accommodate the existing equipment. In any case, there should be sufficient space to allow for growth, particularly in the case of disk storage. Bear in mind, however, the continuing trend towards smaller components.

3.1.1.3 Designing and building the accommodation

Following acceptance of the Full Study report by senior management, the project team should start preparing an Operational Requirement (OR) for the procurement of new equipment, and an Accommodation Design Brief for the specification of the new accommodation. The design of the computer accommodation can now be started, bearing in mind that it will probably take much longer to design and build the accommodation than to purchase the equipment and that the accommodation has to be handed over in a clean state before the equipment can be installed. During the Design and Build phases for a mainframe installation,

Section 3
Planning for computer installation and acceptance

the following management aspects of planning an environment should be considered:

* the selection of environmental standards
* planning acceptance procedures
* interface to the OR
* interface to the Accommodation Design Brief
* managing changes to the plan and/or construction.

The above items are described in detail in the following paragraphs.

The selection of environmental standards

In the past, suppliers of computer equipment were required to define the environmental conditions required by that equipment. As a result, it was not possible to specify the accommodation details until the supplier was known, which was often too late for a timely building programme. To overcome this problem, CCTA introduced a range of standard environmental specifications which were included in the CC88 contract conditions for government purchasers. As CC88 has been replaced by Model Agreements, the Environmental Standards are now included in a Schedule which is appended to the Agreement. Government organizations wishing to use these Model Agreements, should consider which of the optional Environmental Conditions should be incorporated as a Schedule to the System Supply Agreement. These conditions are acceptable to most computer manufacturers and should be included in the Accommodation Design Brief. The appropriate options are:

* Environmental Conditions to be provided by the Authority when full environmental control is to be provided (most suitable for use when installing mainframe computers)

* Environmental Conditions to be provided by the Authority when limited environmental control is to be provided (less stringent control on environmental tolerances for small mainframes and mini-computers)

* Environmental Conditions to be provided by the Authority when equipment is to be installed in UK Government offices (minimum control of conditions in office environments).

The options include standards for temperature and humidity control, dust levels, etc. Guidance on the selection and use of these conditions is given in the IT Infrastructure Library module on **Environmental Standards for Equipment Accommodation**. The advantage of using these conditions is that manufacturers and suppliers are informed of the quality of the accommodation (in terms of environmental conditions and power supply characteristics) that will be available to receive IT equipment. Hence the required environmental conditions can be specified to the accommodation provider before the evaluation of tenders for the IT equipment, thereby reducing the risks that lack of accommodation will delay completion of projects.

Those readers who do not use CCTA's contracts should examine the requirements of their potential suppliers of equipment and specify their environment accordingly.

Planning acceptance procedures

During the design and build phase, consideration should be given to the procedures and criteria which will be used in accepting the accommodation (see also 3.1.1.4). These procedures will include a physical survey of the accommodation to ensure that it meets the required specification; inspections will have to be conducted at various stages in the construction to check that the correct building materials are being used, for instance. Tests will also be required to ensure that the specified environmental conditions can be maintained.

Interface to the Operational Requirement

Both the selected environmental conditions and the acceptance procedures for the equipment should be clearly stated in the Operational Requirement (OR). This is the document which is issued to potential suppliers in order to convey the organization's requirements for IT facilities as defined in the Full Study. The OR should specify the functions to be performed by the equipment (including software) and its performance in use.

Further information is contained in the 'B' set of IS Guides, published by CCTA.

Interface to the Accommodation Design Brief

The Accommodation Design Brief is a detailed specification of the computer accommodation and environmental requirements. Its purpose is to specify these requirements to the building designers. Like the OR, the brief focuses on

what is required, rather than **how** it will be achieved, which is the responsibility of the designers. The structure and contents of the Accommodation Design Brief are described in detail in the IT Infrastructure Library module on **Accommodation Specification**, together with advice on specifying computer accommodation, environment and electrical power requirements.

Many aspects of the Accommodation Design Brief will only become apparent as the procurement proceeds. An obvious example is the cooling arrangements of a mainframe.

It may not be possible to define whether air or water cooling is required until the final hardware configuration is known. Similarly, unless the decision to use distributed or centralized processing is made at an early stage, it will be impossible to describe the accommodation required with any accuracy. Frequent cross-referral to, and updating of, the Accommodation Design Brief is necessary throughout the procurement process to ensure that the design team is made aware of firm requirements as soon as they are known.

Managing changes to the construction

All changes, whether to plans or other documents, such as the Accommodation Design Brief, or to the actual construction, must be controlled by rigorous Change Management procedures. These are described in more detail in section 3.2.3. Everybody involved in the project must be made aware of the procedures and their need to conform to them.

3.1.1.4 Commissioning and testing the accommodation

Before the accommodation is handed over, it should be complete and clean with all plant having been fully commissioned and tested by the contractor. It is at this stage that the Project Manager assumes responsibility for performing acceptance tests to ensure that the accommodation and environment meet the requirements specified in the Accommodation Design Brief. The acceptance tests themselves should have been specified in the Brief. Contingency plans should exist to be actioned in the event of acceptance test failure.

The following aspects (depending on the Environmental Conditions chosen) should be tested to ensure that the requirements are met:

* temperature control
* humidity control
* chilled water/air supplies
* dust levels
* ambient, radiated fields
* electricity supply
* standby electrical power supply
* balancing of electrical supplies
* earthing
* floor resistance
* environmental monitoring equipment.

In order to test some of these it will be necessary to generate an artificial loading in order to simulate normal conditions. For example, the air conditioning should be tested by using a simulated heat load.

Other aspects to be tested include:

* fire precautions, including detection and suppression
* security precautions
* emergency exits
* water detection
* intruder detection.

Further information on accepting computer accommodation is contained in the IT Infrastructure Library module on **Accommodation Specification**.

3.1.1.5 Handover of the computer accommodation

When the acceptance testing has been successfully completed, the acceptance certificate should be signed off and ownership is transferred to the client organization. The accommodation is now ready to receive the equipment. Note that this is a significant milestone, the project should not proceed until it has been signed off.

Section 3
Planning for computer installation and acceptance

3.1.2 Planning to install computer equipment in an existing or new environment

Planning for the installation of new equipment should run in parallel with the preparation for any new accommodation, as described in section 3.1.1.

If new accommodation is not needed, extension or refurbishment of existing accommodation may be required and planning for this should be in place at an early stage. Installation of the equipment will be directly dependent on the availability of the new or refurbished accommodation.

The co-operation of the users during the project is essential. They should be kept informed as the project plans develop and agreement should be sought for their involvement in the project, including participation in the project team, defining future service levels, supporting trials and cut-over plans. Training plans should be established for all users of new equipment and software.

3.1.2.1 Order management

The first task is to identify the equipment needed. For government departments, the Operational Requirement (OR) will invite proposals from potential suppliers which will identify the equipment necessary to meet the requirement. The supplier's reply should be accompanied by bid quotations which respond to the information in the OR. The OR is the principal document used in the procurement process and its use is fully described in the 'B' set of IS Guides and the **Guide to Procurement within the Total Acquisition Process**, all produced by CCTA. Further information on the OR is also contained in section 3.1.1.3.

Many organizations have a procurement function whose responsibility is to purchase equipment. They will assist in producing a list of potential suppliers, using their experience. Non-government organizations should make contact with their procurement function to establish the ordering process, which normally involves a request for quotation to potential suppliers. Further information is contained in Annex C.

While the procurement organization manages the quotation and ordering cycles, the project team should maintain close liaison with them and hold regular, minuted meetings in order to track the status of the ordered equipment.

When the quotation cycle has been completed and the successful suppliers have been identified, an equipment order should be submitted through Procurement. All the contact points of the suppliers, eg Account Manager/Sales, Technical representative, must be known to the project team as frequent contact will be necessary. In addition, lead-times for equipment delivery must be known in detail.

3.1.2.2 Configuration and Change Management

As new hardware and software is ordered, it should be brought under Configuration and Change Management.

Configuration Management

The objective of Configuration Management is to record the name, version and status of items which make up the IT infrastructure. It extends beyond maintaining a simple inventory and asset register containing details of supplier, asset value, depreciation method, etc by recording the relationships between the items and status, eg *on order*. The process must ensure that all changes to the infrastructure are properly authorized and recorded.

Early involvement of Configuration Management staff is essential to ensure that new items are recorded in the Configuration Management database (CMDB) when they are ordered. The status of these items is updated as they are *delivered, installed, tested, accepted*, etc.

At the end of each stage in the project a Configuration Audit should be undertaken to check that the physical configuration items, their status and the relationships between them are correctly reflected in the CMDB.

Further information is contained in the IT Infrastructure Library module on **Configuration Management**.

Change Management

As the project progresses, changes will occur to plans, designs, layouts, key dates and organization. The project team must monitor all such changes and ensure that they can be accommodated within the project plan. If a change management process exists within the IT Services organization, the project team must ensure that all changes are managed through it. If there is no existing change management process, the project team should set one up for the duration of the project. All changes affecting the planning and installation must be documented and signed

Section 3
Planning for computer installation and acceptance

off by the Project Manager. The impact of changes upon existing IT service requirements must be considered to avoid unnecessary disruption.

Further information is contained in section 3.2.3 and in the IT Infrastructure Library module on **Change Management**.

3.1.2.3 Physical layout planning

Layout planning should be conducted by the organization's site planning staff in conjunction with the equipment supplier's installation planning engineers. Computer-aided design (CAD) or other suitable design tools should be used to assist with this work.

Computer Room

Whether the Computer Centre is new or exists already, consideration should be given to the location of new equipment, taking into account:

* access routes, which must be capable of allowing the computer equipment to be easily moved in and out
* clearances between units, including an allowance for maintenance work and cleaning
* raised floor tile cut-outs, which will be required when the new equipment is installed
* ergonomic layout. It may be possible to locate some of the new equipment near to existing similar items, for example, disk drives and tape units, which need operator intervention
* provision for future moves
* cable length restrictions. The supplier's installation planning engineers should be consulted.

Reference should be made to Figure 2, overleaf, which shows an example of a computer room layout.

The computer room plan should be reviewed by the project team to ensure that the following issues have been addressed:

* floor area and shape
* room height
* raised floor loading

The IT Infrastructure Library
Computer Installation and Acceptance

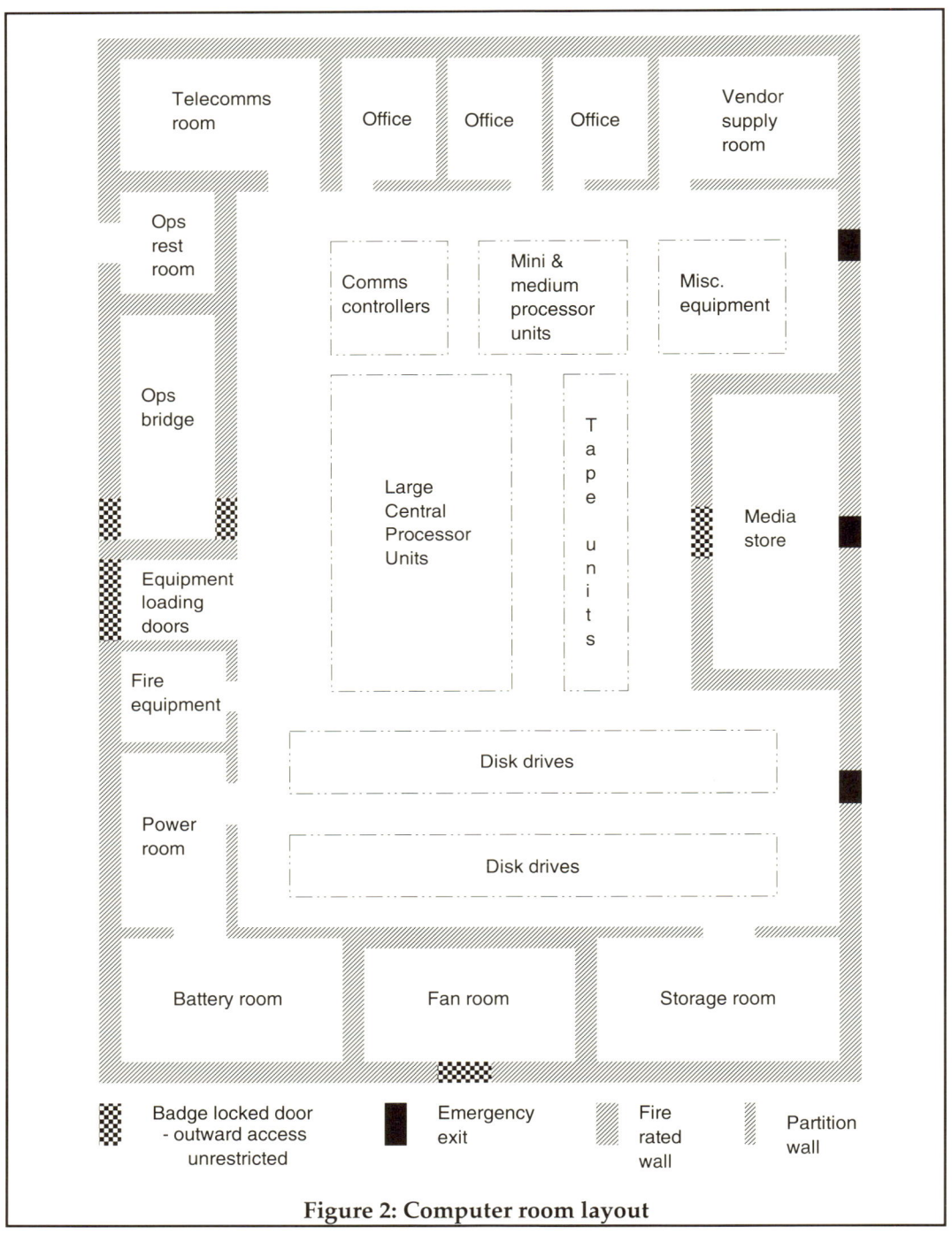

Figure 2: Computer room layout

Section 3
Planning for computer installation and acceptance

* chilled water connections
* placement of air-vents
* electrical and mechanical services
* security requirements
* health and safety requirements.

Delivery schedules should be carefully planned and reviewed to ensure that equipment moves are kept to a minimum. Where continuity of service is required during the installation period, it may be necessary to install temporary equipment to maintain IT services whilst equipment moves take place. If this is the case, additional space (including power and air conditioning) may be required.

Building drawings should be amended to reflect the new layout. Cabling for the equipment will need to be identified and ordered.

Further information is contained in the IT Infrastructure Library modules on **Specification and Management of a Cable Infrastructure**, **Cable Infrastructure Strategy** and **Accommodation Specification**.

Building Access

Consideration must be given as to how the equipment will be brought into the building. This will be particularly relevant if the computer room is not at ground level. Plan the route carefully, taking into consideration equipment size and weight, vehicle access, and liaison with the police if roads are likely to be obstructed. Special lifting equipment may also be necessary.

It is recommended that a site survey be conducted to establish a plan to manage the delivery of the equipment, including storage space for the equipment whilst awaiting installation.

Support areas

Control Room/Bridge — Computer operations should be controlled from an Operations Bridge or control room which may well be outside of the controlled environment of the main computer room. The area accommodates operators and master consoles. An Operations Bridge would also accommodate Network Control and the Help Desk staff. Furniture needs (to office standards) for the control room must be identified and the layout planned. Equipment should include

The IT Infrastructure Library
Computer Installation and Acceptance

telephones, public address system control (see 3.1.2.5), and possibly facsimile and photocopier. If other equipment, such as tape units, is to be installed in the room (not recommended), air-conditioning or additional cooling may be required.

Further information is contained in the IT Infrastructure Library modules on **Computer Operations Management** and **Unattended Operating**.

Telecommunications
: Telecommunications equipment, consisting of termination frames, modems and controllers for internal and external communication lines, is usually located together in a telecommunications room. This room often forms part of the computer room but, if it is separate, air-conditioning may be required. The maximum distance of the room from the computer room will be determined by the maximum allowable length of connecting cables and ergonomic considerations. The size of the room will be dependent on the amount of equipment to be installed.

Furniture needs, etc for this room such as tables, chairs, storage cupboards and telephones, should also be identified.

Media Store
: The environmental conditions of the store for magnetic and optical media must be the same as for the computer room. Tape reels should be stored vertically, in dust proof containers. It is recommended that tapes and cartridges carry a description of the data contained therein and a data classification. There should be a log to record all movements of media in and out of the store. The volume of media to be stored will determine whether a new room, or an extension to an existing one, is needed. Advice should be sought from Computer Operations staff and/or the Capacity Manager on current and future volumes.

Data Entry
: Data entry is increasingly carried out by users, so a specific area for data preparation may not be required. If such a facility is required, its size will depend on the number of people and amount of equipment needed. It will ideally be located near to the computer room. Consideration should be given to the security requirements in relation to the sensitivity and value of the data (see 3.1.2.4).

Further information is contained in the IT Infrastructure Library module on **Computer Operations Management**.

Section 3
Planning for computer installation and acceptance

Engineers' room	It may be necessary to provide facilities for maintenance engineers to store and repair equipment. This does not normally require a controlled environment. Facilities required are:

* a telephone with 24-hour operation for incoming and outgoing calls
* a lockable desk with chair
* a storage cabinet
* a workbench with adjustable light.

Mechanical, electrical and fire protection plant or equipment must not be stored in this room although a fire extinguisher will be required as inflammable cleaning fluids may be kept here.

Printer room	The printer room may be adjacent to the computer room or remote from it, depending on ergonomic considerations. It should be separate from the computer room because of noise and dust levels and preferably air-conditioned. The printer room should be located near goods handling areas and the mail room to allow efficient movement of large volumes of paper. Some printers may be installed in the computer room, depending on service-related printing requirements and the need for operators to service them. However, this may be impractical if an unattended working regime is in operation. There may also be security considerations for the placement of printers, eg for printing cheques or classified information. In addition to the above, printing facilities are likely to be required in the user work areas.
Bulk stationery store	Paper stores should be adjacent to the printing machines and goods inwards/outwards to reduce the movement of large volumes of paper. The store must be protected from extremes of temperature and humidity.

3.1.2.4 Security

General Guidance

Consideration must be given to the security of all areas associated with data processing. Equipment will need to be protected from deliberate and accidental disruption to its availability. Certain sensitive or classified data may require special security controls to maintain its confidentiality and integrity.

Access to areas containing essential engineering services, such as transformers and switchgear, should be strictly controlled.

During the building and installation activities, it will be necessary for suppliers to visit the site. A plan should be in place for these visits to be arranged, through Procurement, with the Departmental Security Officer and IT Security Officer involved. They should ensure that the security countermeasures, which have been determined by risk analysis reviews, are implemented.

In government departments the Project Manager must consult the Departmental Security Officer at an early stage to seek general physical security implementation guidance. Non-government organizations should contact their security departments.

Subject to the recommendations from a security risk analysis review, several different types of physical security control may be considered.

Badge reader

This type of access control is the most flexible. Access to secure areas can be limited to prearranged times of the day by means of a plastic card with a data-encoded magnetic strip.

This degree of control gives added security in the event of a card being lost or stolen, as access can be quickly revoked. Other support staff, including cleaners and maintenance personnel, can be allocated shorter periods for their activities. More sophisticated systems can keep a record of each entry and exit.

Closed circuit television (CCTV)

CCTV provides visual monitoring of sensitive areas and may be considered where full-time security personnel are present. Cameras can be installed inside and outside buildings. Sites without full-time cover can be monitored by video recorders.

CCTV systems are expensive and movement detectors may be considered more appropriate for small or unoccupied computer rooms.

Section 3
Planning for computer installation and acceptance

Other means of access control

For smaller rooms, electronic programmable key locks may be used. The disadvantage of this method is that the combination may become known by unauthorised personnel and it is necessary to change the combination frequently to maintain security.

Electrically-operated locks, especially on escape routes, must fail safe to the open position in the event of power failure, to allow emergency exits to be used.

Double, interlocked doors may be considered, which provide additional control against 'tailgating' and an air lock to assist in maintaining environmental room conditions.

Media Protection

Data is often sensitive or classified and of considerable value. Detection and prevention of unauthorised removal of media containing this data should be considered. Systems using magnetic sensors at entry and exit points, similar to those used in retail stores, are a means of providing protection. For optical media, appropriate means of detection should be used, such as tags or random searches. A separate secure location should be provided for back-up media.

Support areas

If the raised floor void in a sensitive area extends to other, less secure areas, barriers must be provided under the floor, in the form of mesh or other suitable material, to prevent access.

Fire precautions

Computer rooms should be located away from areas vulnerable to high fire-risk such as kitchens. Large computer rooms should be separated from other areas by 2-hour rated fire walls, with openings protected by 1-hour rated self closing fire doors. Smaller computer rooms need to be separated from other areas by half-hour rated partitions or walls and self closing doors.

All construction materials, pipework, ducts, cables, conduits, trunking, trays and insulation must be non-flammable or, where appropriate, low-smoke and fume materials should be used.

Further information is contained in the IT Infrastructure Library module on **Fire Precautions in IT Installations**.

Flood precautions

Consideration must be given to vulnerability to flooding, first when choosing the site and secondly during the design phase. Computer rooms should be sited away from reservoirs and rivers, and the building should be designed so that water cannot enter from above, eg from a poorly maintained flat roof or overhead water tanks.

Incident reporting

Any incident involving security should be reported to the IT Security Officer immediately.

Further information

Further information on security matters can be found in the CCTA IS Guide C4: **Security and Privacy**.

3.1.2.5 Health and Safety

General Guidance

The current edition of the Health and Safety at Work Etc Act and other relevant statutory requirements apply to all personnel designing, constructing, operating and maintaining computer equipment.

Safe working practices must be used and all work performed in such a way that no safety hazard is present or likely to arise. Health and safety policies and procedures must be defined and observed.

Public Address (PA) systems

Computer rooms and associated areas will normally have a PA system installed as part of fire precautions. These systems can be used where telephones are impractical or in emergency situations such as fire or bomb threat.

Site safety

Access routes to machines must be safe and without risk to health. Safety practices and procedures should be clearly displayed in a prominent position.

The significance of emergency and warning alarms must be defined and consequent action specified. Emergency exits and escape routes need to be clearly defined and indicated. If there are special clothing requirements, their usage should be defined.

Section 3
Planning for computer installation and acceptance

Workstations

All workstations, such as those in operations bridges or data entry facilities, installed after 1 January 1993 must comply with the **Health and Safety (Display Screen Equipment) Regulations, 1992**. This lays down minimum requirements for protecting the health and safety of workers by ensuring that all aspects of a workstation are properly designed and used.

A workstation includes:

* the VDU and accessories
* the keyboard
* disk drive, printer, modem, telephone
* desk/worksurface, document holder, chair
* immediate work environment
* the software interface.

Electrical Safety

The electrical installation must comply with the requirements of relevant safety standards. It is recommended that periodic checks are conducted to verify the safe earthing of machines.

Further information is contained in the **IEE Regulations for Electrical Installations** and Annex D.

Incident reporting

Any incident or 'near miss' involving personnel or machines should be promptly reported to the site Safety Officer, at the time of occurrence.

3.1.2.6 Planning implementation

As part of planning for the installation of hardware and software, a team of operations and technical services personnel should be identified. This team will be involved in preparing for the equipment delivery and planning for acceptance and will act in support of the project team. The following items should be considered at this stage, a check list is contained in Annex E.

New hardware

The Project Manager should ensure that plans are in place to:

* verify that the physical layout will be completed in time for the arrival of the new equipment

* receive the new equipment and documentation

* unpack the equipment and deliver it to the Computer Centre, having verified that all items ordered have been received

* have building drawings available to indicate positioning of the equipment

* have cut-out floor tiles available to allow the machine cabling to be passed through the raised floor to connection points

* establish if any changes need to be applied to the delivered hardware

* ensure that the supplier's Installation Engineers will be available when required.

New software

The Project Manager should ensure that plans are in place to:

* check that all items of software received are as ordered, including supporting documentation

* check that all new software is properly licensed

* establish whether any changes need to be applied to the delivered software

* check that external support to the installation is available, if required

* ensure that Operations staff are available to support the installation

* merge existing software with new software.

Further information is contained in the IT Infrastructure Library modules on **Testing an IT Service for Operational Use** and **Software Control and Distribution**.

Section 3
Planning for computer installation and acceptance

Communications Equipment

If an existing computer centre is being moved, plans to provide temporary communications devices such as modems and controllers will need to be considered. Additionally, upgrades to existing communication controllers may be necessary. In either case, continuity of IT services during the installation period may need to be preserved.

Operations

The installation of new hardware and software will affect Computer Operations. Plans should be in place to ensure that they are aware of the new equipment and its operation. They should provide input to the acceptance criteria.

Further information is contained in the IT Infrastructure Library module on **Computer Operations Management**.

Parallel running

It may be necessary for existing hardware and software to continue operation during the installation period. The Project Manager should ensure that plans are in place to continue providing existing services, with the use of temporary equipment and staff, if necessary.

Where existing applications are to be transferred to the new installation, plans should be made for the cut-over.

Decommissioning of equipment

It is possible that the installation will replace existing equipment and software. The decommissioning and removal of the replaced equipment and software should be reflected in cut-over plans, which should be completed before handover. Cut-over planning needs to be carried out with extreme care to ensure that existing services are not affected by the new installation, eg it should take place during a weekend if possible, or other off-peak time. In any case cut-over plans must include procedures to keep all affected staff, including users, fully informed.

3.1.2.7 Planning acceptance

The acceptance policy should be planned, eg unit testing, integration testing, system testing. Will any of the applications under development be ready to run when the equipment is installed? If so, these applications will be available for acceptance testing and can be specified as such and agreed with the supplier, see section B1 of Annex B for further information. If no suitable applications will be ready, some other means of testing the equipment must be found. It may be possible to simulate the new applications by constructing some simplified prototypes with, for example, a fourth generation language. However, be aware that some 4GLs have greatly different performance and storage characteristics to third generation languages. If there is an existing system, it may be possible to transfer a copy of it to the new equipment for acceptance testing.

At a time specified in the supply contract, before the start of the pre-defined acceptance period, an acceptance testing schedule should be agreed with the supplier. The schedule should include:

* the acceptance timetable, to include the start and end dates with key milestones in between

* workload details, including specific tests and any benchmark jobs to be run. These tests should be of known function and performance

* any demonstrations required during the acceptance period

* system or unit configuration, including any required media and consumables

* Minimum Trial System

* acceptance criteria - functionality, performance, serviceability, security

* incident reporting procedures

* staffing to operate the trial system

* a record of the items under test.

For users of the CCTA Draft Contract procedures, a Schedule to the Model System Supply Agreement deals with the preparation for, and performance of, acceptance procedures. Another Schedule describes the actual acceptance procedures and acceptance criteria. These schedules are fully explained in Annex B.

Section 3
Planning for computer installation and acceptance

Communications Equipment

Liaison with the suppliers of communications equipment and lines is necessary to ensure that the delivery of these items is synchronized with the other equipment and that all relevant equipment required for the trials is in place. This might include:

* communication circuits - LANs and WANs
* modems, multiplexors, gateways, bridges
* patch panels and modem racks
* communication controllers
* network monitors.

The cabling throughout the building and network needs to be completed for the acceptance trials. Cabling may be required for the following devices:

* terminals
* printers
* word processors
* microcomputers
* plotters.

Plans should be in place to have telephones and facsimile machines installed to support the acceptance trials.

3.1.2.8 Planning for ongoing management

Plans must be made for the ongoing operation and management of the computer centre, for example:

* management of IT services
* a plan for the disposal of any replaced and temporary equipment
* a plan to hand over the computer room to IT Services Management
* a plan to implement user support facilities, including a Help Desk. This should be located with the Operations Bridge. Further information is contained in the IT Infrastructure Library modules on **Help Desk** and **Problem Management**

* project evaluation review. The primary objective of this review will be to ensure that the installation, testing and subsequent handover to Computer Operations was completed as planned. Lessons learned from the project should be included in the review and recorded for future reference. The review success criteria should be planned at this time.

Further information can be obtained in section 5.

3.2 Dependencies

This section describes those activities upon which the planning phase is dependent.

Successful planning is dependent on:

* identification of all activities and tasks
* accurate estimates of resources required
* co-operation of and communication with staff.

Delivery of new systems and services may be dependent on new hardware. Contingency should be built into the plans to allow for possible delays.

3.2.1 Project funding

The approval of finances is crucial to the timely completion of the project. Financial planning for the project should include the following:

* the cost of all staff involved in the project, including training
* the purchase or rental of any equipment needed to support the project and trials, including consumables
* the cost of running the trial system
* parallel running costs, including the use of temporary equipment.

This approval can often be a slow process, so adequate time should be allowed before the start of the project. It should be borne in mind that there is a general tendency to underestimate the funding, time and resources needed to complete a project.

3.2.2 Project management tools and techniques

It is recommended that the management of the Installation and Acceptance project is performed in accordance with a recognized project management method, such as PRINCE.

A large complex project is difficult to plan and manage without effective software tools. There will be a large number of tasks and a large number of people involved. The timing of the tasks will be related to the availability of the people assigned to perform them. Regular, minuted meetings must be held to track the progress of the project. These meetings will require progress reports which compare actual costs and timescales against those planned. The Project Manager should keep the Project Board informed of status, particularly if there is a likelihood of slippage in the schedule. Where slippage occurs, the tool will be required to reschedule the project. The overall objective is to maintain control of all project activities. Further information is contained in the IS Guide A5 - **A Project Manager's Guide** produced by CCTA, and in section 7 of this module.

3.2.3 Configuration and Change Management

A major dependency for a successful project is Configuration Management. All items to be supplied, eg hardware, software, cabling, documentation, should be recorded in a Configuration Management database as soon as they are ordered. The hierarchical relationships between them should also be recorded wherever possible. This enables the impact of a change upon any associated items to be determined. The status of each item should be updated as it is delivered, installed, tested, accepted, etc (see also 3.1.2.2).

All changes to be made during the project, whether to the IT infrastructure or project plans and documents, should be subject to the Change Management process. Briefly, this means the raising and logging of a formal Request for Change (RFC) for each change. Once an RFC has been received by the Project Change Manager, the Change Advisory Board (in this case, the project team) should:

* authorize (or not) each RFC
* decide on priorities

The IT Infrastructure Library
Computer Installation and Acceptance

* assess the impact and the resource requirements
* assess the cost of the change
* schedule each change.

The Change Manager is responsible for ensuring that all changes are:

* tested
* formally accepted
* implemented as scheduled
* reviewed after implementation.

3.2.4 Problem Management

Throughout the project, problems will be identified. To ensure that these problems are visible to all concerned, and not concealed or lost, they should be recorded by a Problem Management process and followed through to a satisfactory conclusion. Since a solution often involves making a change, there must be a close relationship between the Change and Problem Management processes. It is recommended that problem and change records are kept on the same Configuration Management database to improve the ability to cross-refer.

3.2.5 Acceptance plans

As described in section 3.1.2.7, an acceptance plan should be in place which will define the acceptance procedures and criteria. Workloads must be available which will test the hardware, communications equipment, software and applications to the satisfaction of the Project Manager.

3.3 People

The key people involved during the planning phase of the project are described in the following sections, 3.3.1 to 3.3.7.

3.3.1 IT Services Manager

The IT Services Manager has overall responsibility for the quality of services delivered. The IT Services Manager should initiate the process of installation and acceptance of new equipment and take overall responsibility for its successful outcome. The Project Manager reports to the IT Services Manager.

3.3.2 Project Board

The purpose of the Project Board is to ensure that the project and its constituent stages are managed effectively. The Project Board should consist of senior managers, each representing major project interests: namely, executive, user and technical. It is probable that the IT Director will be the chairman of the project board. The composition of the project board must reflect the importance of the project and the commitment of senior management to the successful installation of the new equipment.

Further information is contained in the IS Guide A5, **A Project Manager's Guide** and the **PRINCE** manuals.

3.3.3 Project Manager

The Project Manager will be appointed by the Project Board and report to the IT Services Manager. This should be a full time post for the duration of the project, which will end when the equipment is installed and handed over to Computer Operations. For this reason the Operations Manager designate is often chosen as the Project Manager (at least on a greenfield site). However, it should be noted that project management skills should be the main selection criterion for this post. Providing computer accommodation and installing equipment is a very complex operation, which must be carefully planned and executed to agreed timescales and budget. Failure to do so will mean that an organization will not be able to carry out the business activities which depend on the equipment being installed. The Project Manager must have a broad understanding of the organization's business, good attention to detail and sufficient stature within the organization to be able to motivate all those involved in the project.

The Project Manager should ensure that good communications and working relationships are maintained among all parties involved in the project. Many organizations expect contractors, whether they are computer suppliers or builders, to take primary responsibility for the project. It should be borne in mind that the Project Manager bears the day-to-day responsibility for the success of the project and that it is the organization's business which is at stake. However, it should not be necessary to view contractors as adversaries or keep them at arm's length in a supplier/purchaser relationship. The aim should be to create a partnership with contractors and a climate of mutual trust in which frank and easy communication is encouraged. A successful project is in everyone's interest.

The IT Infrastructure Library
Computer Installation and Acceptance

Further information is contained in the IT Infrastructure Library module on **Managing Supplier Relationships**.

3.3.4 Project team

It is essential that IT Services is represented in the project and sub-project teams. Involvement will be required from the following functions at various times throughout the project:

* Service Level Management
* Change Management
* Problem Management
* Configuration Management
* Capacity Management
* Network Management
* Operations Management
* Contingency Planning.

Involvement will also be required from other internal functions such as:

* Procurement
* Security
* Office Services
* representatives from the users.

Architects, quantity surveyors, computer suppliers, cabling specialists, mechanical and electrical engineers and fit-out subcontractors will also be required as necessary.

The role of the project team is to ensure that the installation, acceptance testing and subsequent handover are successfully completed to plan.

3.3.5 Suppliers

The involvement of suppliers of all the systems and services will be required throughout the planning phase. Their input will be essential in estimating the resources required and timescales for many of the activities. They will be involved in the planning for the delivery and acceptance of equipment.

Section 3
Planning for computer installation and acceptance

3.3.6 Support staff

3.3.6.1 Operators

It is important for computer operations staff to be involved at an early stage to allow them adequate time to become familiar with the new environment. Current operating procedures should be amended and, where necessary, new ones written. Operations staff should be actively involved during the acceptance testing as this will probably be their first opportunity to work with the new equipment. Staff training is covered in section 3.3.9.

Further information is contained in the IT Infrastructure Library module on **Computer Operations Management**.

3.3.6.2 Hardware planners

Hardware planners may be permanent staff, suppliers or consultants. They should be involved in the project at the physical layout planning stage and will be the source of advice and guidance to the project team from this time onwards.

3.3.6.3 Systems programmers

Systems programmers must have information concerning all new systems software and applications. They should be actively involved in specifying and procuring equipment, planning acceptance, assist in defining the test plan and be involved in the software trials. Their involvement is essential, as they will provide the primary support for systems software when the installation is completed.

3.3.7 Others involved

3.3.7.1 Procurement staff

Procurement is one of the contacts between the organization and the supplier. Procurement staff will be involved with the planning staff in drawing up and issuing the OR and Accommodation Design Brief. They will be responsible for progressing the procurement of accommodation and equipment and must maintain regular contact with the project team until all of the equipment is on-site. Procurement should take action if there are any problems with the contractual timetables for accommodation or equipment.

3.3.7.2 Security staff

Government departments have a Departmental Security Officer who must be consulted for general security guidance. Non-government organizations should contact their security departments.

More technical advice on security matters in relation to specific threats and risks associated with the computer room, equipment, data, etc, should be obtained from the IT Security Officer.

3.3.7.3 Office services

Office services must be involved in the planning of new buildings. They should be responsible for all new telephone requirements, mail delivery points, changes to directories and new office equipment and furniture needs, including removals. They will be expected to manage the purchasing and implementation of these facilities.

3.3.7.4 Users

Users must be represented on the project team. Their requirements, eg for functionality, performance, timescales, will have to be taken into account and reflected in the OR. They will be required to assist in developing and participating in acceptance tests. The user community must be kept informed as the Computer Centre develops. A series of meetings or workshops should be held to involve the users in the planning and its effect on them. Items which should be considered for discussion and agreement include:

* an overview of the new equipment and software
* actions required by the users
* training needs
* user involvement in parallel running
* user participation in acceptance trials
* service level requirements.

3.3.8 Recruitment

In the case of a new computer centre, additional staff will probably have to be recruited. Thought should be given to the functions, roles and skills required. The time needed to recruit new staff ought not to be underestimated as the interviewing and staff selection process can often take several months. Advice and guidance should be sought from the Personnel department.

Section 3
Planning for computer installation and acceptance

If new equipment is being installed in an existing computer centre, recruitment of new staff may not be necessary. However, it may be necessary to hire or borrow staff for the duration of the project, including parallel running. Assigned staff and their management must be clear about their responsibilities and the period involved. It is wise to document the details of the assignment.

If existing roles are being changed as a result of the installation, terms and conditions of employment may need to be reviewed, including amendment of job descriptions and objectives. If staff are required to operate a shift system, the pay section will need to be informed of changes to employee payments. Again, Personnel may be involved in this process. Consultation with Trade Unions will be necessary if employee terms and conditions are likely to be changed.

Further information is contained in the IT Infrastructure Library modules on **Computer Operations Management** and **IT Services Organization**.

3.3.9 Training

Training for staff should consist of formal courses and on-the-job experience. The training must be planned so that it can be completed in line with the implementation schedule. If suppliers offer suitable training facilities, these should be considered for inclusion in the programme.

Training needs will vary, depending on the levels of experience of staff, but as a minimum should cover the new hardware, software, applications and supporting tools. The training of senior operations staff should be given priority as they will be involved in the subsequent training of junior operators, especially on the job training.

Training should be considered for the following groups of people:

* computer operators
* help desk staff
* application programmers
* systems programmers
* technical support
* security officers
* users

The IT Infrastructure Library
Computer Installation and Acceptance

* backup staff
* staff involved in the project implementation review
* site services
* staff involved in conducting acceptance trials.

3.3.10 Overtime and extended hours during acceptance

In planning the introduction of new equipment, IT Services management should consider the need for overtime, shift working or extended hours. This type of working will more likely apply to operations staff, but it may be necessary for other support and project staff to work such patterns. Overtime and shift working can be expensive and the need to operate in this way must be considered very carefully.

3.4 Timing

3.4.1 Project duration

It is estimated that a large computer complex requires approximately two years from conception to completion. Obviously, if equipment only is being installed, less time is needed, but it could still involve a period of nine to twelve months. The overall project plan must identify key milestones and timescales, which should be rigorously measured and reported against. The need to match the building activities to the procurement of the equipment cannot be overstated. The expectations of IT Services management and the users must be constantly borne in mind by the project team.

If the computer centre is new, adequate time must be allowed to introduce service management disciplines such as Configuration Management.

3.4.2 Equipment lead times

Lead times for the supply of equipment can be extensive, particularly if multiple suppliers are involved. The need to co-ordinate equipment delivery through Procurement is extremely important. Failure to meet the expected delivery dates will affect the schedule.

Section 3
Planning for computer installation and acceptance

3.4.3 Staff training

Experience has shown that training of operational and user staff requires a period of several months in order for them to become effective. It will depend on the availability of an instructor, classroom facilities and the ability to gain practical experience on suitable equipment. The training period may extend beyond the handover date. However, sufficient training must have been completed to allow operators and users to be competent in the use of the new equipment by the time it comes into full operation.

The IT Infrastructure Library
Computer Installation and Acceptance

Section 4
Implementation

4. Implementation

This section contains guidance on implementing the plans for the installation and acceptance of new computer equipment, which were described in section 3. The project team is responsible for ensuring that these plans are implemented and that the timing is in line with the commitments made to IT Services Management and the users.

4.1 Procedures

By the implementation phase, the computer accommodation should have been handed over and be available to receive the new equipment. The project team should satisfy themselves that the accommodation is complete and clean. Further information is contained in the IT Infrastructure Library module on **Accommodation Specification**, and in section 3.1.1 of this module.

The accommodation for support staff, described in section 3.1.2.3, should also be ready for use.

Implementation of the plans described in section 3 involves:

* receiving the new equipment and software (4.1.1, see also sections 3.1.2.1 and 3.1.2.6)

* installing the new hardware (4.1.2, see also section 3.1.2.6)

* installing the new software (4.1.3, see also section 3.1.2.7)

* conducting acceptance tests (4.1.4, see also section 3.1.2.6)

* ensuring that service management disciplines are in place (4.1.5, see also section 3.2.3)

* handover of the equipment to IT Services Management (4.1.6, see also section 3.1.2.8)

* ensuring that security plans are implemented (4.1.7, see also section 3.1.2.4)

* ensuring that Health and Safety programmes are in place (4.1.8, see also section 3.1.2.5).

The IT Infrastructure Library
Computer Installation and Acceptance

4.1.1 Receiving new equipment and software

The Project Manager should be satisfied that all new equipment and software is delivered on time and as ordered. The delivery checks should also ensure that supporting documentation, eg invoices, delivery notes, reference material, and that all cables are present. It may not be possible to check the physical existence of software until the equipment is sufficiently usable to be able to read the magnetic media on which the software has been delivered. In this case, at least check the delivery note which should accompany the software. The contract should be used as a reference. If there are any deficiencies, Procurement should be involved in resolving them. The Project Manager should confirm satisfactory receipt of each item to the Configuration Manager, who will ensure that they are recorded on the Configuration Management database and their status updated to *delivered*. Further information is contained in the IT Infrastructure Library module on **Configuration Management**.

Arrangements should be made to unpack and deliver the new equipment to its appropriate accommodation. Unpacking should take place outside of the computer room to avoid contaminating the clean environment. Delivery may be to a temporary storage area, if there is to be a delay in installation. Magnetic media should be stored in a controlled environment for acclimatization.

It is essential that the Problem and Change Management processes are operational at this stage to maintain a record and status of all problems and changes occurring, until the equipment is handed over. These records will be necessary when the post implementation review, which is covered in section 5.1.2, is conducted.

4.1.2 Installation of new hardware

When the new equipment has been delivered to its accommodation, it should be positioned as indicated in the floor and cabling plans. Site services engineers should be present to assist with the positioning and connection of the hardware to the electrical, mechanical and cooling services, as appropriate. Tile cut-outs will be required to allow the machine cabling to be passed through the raised floor to connection points.

Section 4
Implementation

Hardware installation and power-on checks will normally be conducted by the contractor's Installation Engineers, but should be supervised by a member of the project team. The Project Manager should confirm that the checks have been completed satisfactorily. Interconnecting cables should be fitted to associated hardware, such as disk drives, communications controllers, channels and central processors. It is possible that the hardware will be delivered with engineering changes to be fitted. The project Change Manager should ascertain why these changes are required and confirm when they have been correctly installed. The contractors must conform to the project's change management procedures.

When individual items of hardware have been installed and successfully powered on, system checks can be conducted. These consist of power checks of the central processing unit (CPU) and associated units. Basic diagnostic programs should be run to ensure that the CPU can communicate with the equipment attached to it. All of the new equipment should be covered by these checks. Emergency power-off circuits should be tested for each unit installed and for the total system. Alternative paths to tape units, disk drives, channels, controllers and other CPUs should be tested. Other tests, agreed between the project team and the supplier, may be conducted, to demonstrate that the installation has been successfully completed. Operations staff should be involved with these tests. Further information on acceptance trials for those using the CCTA procurement procedures is contained at Annex B.

Other activities which should be considered at this time include:

* the physical layout plans, covered in section 3.1.2.3, should be reviewed to check the physical installation

* the project team should ensure that the Configuration Manager is kept informed as the installation progresses so that records reflect the current status of each item

* parallel running and decommissioning activities should be conducted as appropriate.

Reference should be made to the plans described in section 3.1.2.6.

4.1.3 Installation of new software

Systems and applications software for larger processors will, in most cases, be installed by the systems programmers. Where there are no systems programming staff, or they do not yet possess the necessary skills, the supplier or a third party may be the installer. The project team should liaise with the installer to ensure that any necessary changes have been received and that supporting documentation is available. If software amendments are to be applied, authority for the changes must be sought from the Change Manager. The reasons for the changes should be understood by the project team and details given to the Configuration and Change Managers. The installer must conform to the project's change management procedures.

All software items, both systems and applications, should already be recorded in the Configuration Management database. However, some more work may be required to assign the relationships between the configuration items. Where automated software control and distribution facilities exist (especially useful in a distributed environment), they should be invoked. Otherwise manual procedures should be used to install the software. The status of these software configuration items must now be altered to *installed*. Operations staff should be involved with the software installation as this will be a good opportunity for them to gain an early awareness of the new programs.

Reference should be made to the plans described in section 3.1.2.6.

4.1.4 Acceptance testing

Before acceptance testing, the hardware and software should have been installed and the power-on and diagnostic tests carried out to the satisfaction of the Project Manager. The project team should review any unresolved installation problems and be satisfied that they are of low severity and unlikely to impact the acceptance trials. The Project Manager is responsible for ensuring that all unresolved problems have been assigned for action with a target date for completion. The Availability and Capacity Managers should be involved to ensure that projected serviceability and performance targets can be achieved.

Section 4
Implementation

Acceptance trial procedures and conditions will have been agreed as part of the contract. The purpose of the trial is to demonstrate that:

* the system is complete and free from cosmetic defects
* the facilities of the system or unit under trial are available and function correctly
* performance and serviceability, specified in the contract, is achieved
* output data is produced as expected.

Acceptance testing will include the following processes:

* physical examination of the system and documentation
* functionality tests, including performance
* workload trials, including performance and serviceability.

The trials should be monitored by the project team and a record kept of:

* elapsed time
* predefined performance measurements, eg response times
* serviceability measurements, eg trial system and unit downtime, the time when the system is operating correctly
* environmental conditions, eg temperature, humidity
* all operational activities, including all problems raised and changes made.

Further information is contained in Annex B.

All tests including demonstrations, should be completed to the satisfaction of the Project Manager. These tests should be run by the purchasing organization's operations staff with systems programmers in attendance. Any incidents which occur during the trials should be recorded in the Problem Management system and changes identified as necessary. The Problem, Change and Configuration Managers must be involved as problems occur and changes are made.

When all tests have been completed, the Project Manager should decide if the success criteria have been achieved. Remedial actions or retests, arising from failures, should be completed to the satisfaction of the Project Manager and verified as being within the success criteria. The Project Manager should provide written confirmation of the trial results to the contractor. If the trials were unsuccessful, the Project Manager must consider the contractual position (in consultation with Procurement) and decide if retests are to be conducted or whether the trials are to be abandoned. The wider implications of either course of action must also be considered.

Reference should be made to the plans described in section 3.1.2.6.

4.1.5 Associated disciplines

4.1.5.1 Operations

Some operational staff will have been involved in the installation and acceptance trials and should have a good understanding of the new equipment and software. Plans to train other operations staff should now be implemented.

Operating procedures should have been written or amended, including recovery procedures. The Operations Manager should be preparing to accept the new equipment into normal day-to-day running. The Operations Manager should also verify that the operations control room has been completed as planned.

Further information is contained in the IT Infrastructure Library module on **Computer Operations Management**.

4.1.5.2 Configuration and Change Management

As new equipment and software arrives on the site, its introduction into any existing infrastructure should be managed through Configuration and Change Management. These functions should assess the impact and any risks involved in new equipment being introduced into the infrastructure.

The Configuration Manager should ensure that the Configuration Management database reflects new equipment and software delivered and all relevant changes made during the installation and acceptance periods.

The Change Manager should ensure that all changes authorized during the installation and acceptance periods have been satisfactorily implemented. If changes are still to be implemented, the Project Manager should be consulted to establish if acceptance sign-off is likely to be affected.

Further information is contained in section 3.1.2.2.

4.1.5.3 Help Desk/Problem Management

The Help Desk should be in place, including any training of staff and users. The Help Desk should have copies of supporting documentation, including manuals and relevant program listings, to assist with first-level problem determination after handover.

The Problem Manager should be satisfied either that all problems raised during the installation and acceptance periods are resolved or that resolution action is in progress. High-severity, unresolved problems should be discussed with the Project Manager, as they may affect acceptance sign-off.

Further information is contained in the IT Infrastructure Library module on **Problem Management**.

4.1.5.4 Contingency Planning

Contingency procedures must be in place and should include the following:

* identification of personnel with the authority to initiate recovery procedures

* procedures which clearly identify recovery actions

* a backup location, preferably at another site

* backup equipment and facilities needed in the event of a disaster

* off-site storage of essential data, which should include backup copies of all software, data and documentation

* agreement to the contingency plans by all relevant parties, including the backup location

* contracts with providers of disaster recovery facilities and/or documents of understanding for the emergency supply of replacement equipment

The IT Infrastructure Library
Computer Installation and Acceptance

* contingency arrangements should be reflected in Service Level Agreements (SLAs)
* contingency test plans.

Further information is contained in the IT Infrastructure Library module on **Contingency Planning**.

4.1.5.5 Service Level Management

Services to be delivered by the new systems should be defined in SLAs between IT Services and representatives of the users. The Service Level Manager, in conjunction with the Capacity Manager and the Availability Manager, should be involved in the acceptance process. They should check that the performance and serviceability criteria have been met and that the SLAs can be supported by the new systems.

Further information is contained in the IT Infrastructure Library module on **Service Level Management**.

4.1.6 Equipment handover

Prior to handover an awareness campaign should be carried out to publicise the handover and availability of services to all interested users. This is a good opportunity to make the users aware not only of new services but also of the benefits to be gained from the use of those services.

Equipment will normally be handed over from the project team to IT Services Management after the following activities have been completed:

* running of all trials and tests
* resolution of outstanding problems
* implementation of authorized changes
* formal sign-off of the installation and acceptance.

The plans to cut over existing equipment and services (see section 3.1.2.6) should be implemented.

At the end of any parallel running, any temporary or superseded equipment used should be decommissioned and removed. Any associated maintenance contracts or software licences should be cancelled.

4.1.7 Security

Security arrangements, outlined in section 3.1.2.4, should be in place with supporting written procedures. The Departmental Security Officer should be satisfied that these procedures are documented, tested, operable and clear in order that people and assets are properly protected. Security implementation should be signed off by the appropriate Security Officer. Security clearances should be reviewed before suppliers and contractors leave the site.

4.1.8 Health and Safety

Health and Safety procedures and practices, outlined in section 3.1.2.5, should be in place and signed off by the Safety Officer. Practices should cover local personnel and any contractors remaining on the site after handover.

4.2 Dependencies

Successful installation is dependent on the following:

* acceptance of plans by IT Services Management
* computer accommodation which is fit for the intended purpose and available at the right time
* prompt delivery of equipment and software, including supporting documentation and cables
* prompt solution of problems by suppliers
* availability of appropriately skilled people
* a successful publicity and awareness campaign
* network activities completed
* environmental activities completed
* training completed for
    - operational staff
    - Help Desk staff
    - programmers and hardware support staff
    - user staff.

4.3 People

Support staff, covered in section 3.3.6, should assume post-handover responsibility.

4.3.1 Operations staff

Operations staff should support the installation and acceptance trials and will assume full operational responsibility after handover. The Operations Manager should ensure that all training is completed and that staff are capable of assuming this responsibility. Further information is contained in the IT Infrastructure Library module on **Computer Operations Management**.

4.3.2 Systems Programmers

The systems programmers should now be thoroughly familiar with the new systems and applications software and be capable of providing support. They will normally act as a second level of support to the Operations and Help Desk staff. Program listings should be available to systems programmers to assist in fault diagnosis.

4.3.3 Hardware support

Day-to-day hardware support will normally be provided by the maintenance engineers in accordance with the maintenance agreement. Unresolved problems will be referred to them by the Problem Manager. Any hardware modifications required to clear the problems must be subject to the change management procedures.

4.4 Timing

The timing of implementation will be as specified in the Project plan. Considerations which may have a bearing on bringing the new systems into service are:

* business needs, including commitments made to external bodies, such as
    - availability of Electronic Data Interchange connections
    - service support to new legislation, eg tax regulations

Section 4
Implementation

* monetary, including the availability of funds and the impact of financial year-end
* operational services, including the availability of electrical, mechanical and chilled water facilities
* availability of skilled people
* holidays; if a shut-down period is operated, this may be a practical time to install and accept new equipment
* acceptance trial period, which should be as specified in the supply contract.

The IT Infrastructure Library
Computer Installation and Acceptance

Section 5
Post-implementation and audit

5. Post-implementation and audit

The purpose of this section is to describe review and audit processes that are required after handover of the new equipment. The objective of these processes is to keep operations and service management systems under regular review and ensure that they are complying with the agreed procedures. The review and audit activities should interface with the Problem and Change Management procedures, to ensure that outstanding actions are properly followed up.

Ongoing management of the services is based on the plans described in section 3.1.2.8.

5.1 Procedures

5.1.1 Project evaluation review

A project evaluation review should be conducted immediately after handover by one or two members from the project team, before it is disbanded. The objectives of this review will be to evaluate whether:

* plans and timetables were realistic
* planned goals and targets of the project, identified in the Project Initiation Document, were met
* cost and resource estimates were reasonable
* control procedures were effective.

It is important that the lessons learned from the project are identified and documented, for future reference. The success factors defined during the planning stage should be reviewed against the achievement. It is appropriate for some of the original project team to undertake this work, as they will be familiar with the planning and implementation phases.

On completion, a project evaluation report should be written, to include the activities reviewed, conclusions and recommendations for improvement. The report should be submitted to the project closure meeting attended by the Project Board, the Project Manager, the Stage Manager of the final stage and the Project Assurance Team. Further information is contained in the 'A' set of IS guides, especially **A Project Manager's Guide**.

5.1.2 Post-implementation review

A post-implementation review should be conducted between six and twelve months after handover, by a team of two or three people from the operations or systems support areas and will require co-operation and liaison with the following staff:

* Service Level Management
* Capacity Management
* Problem Management
* Change Management
* Configuration Management
* IT Services Manager
* Departmental Security Officer.

The objectives of this review will be to ascertain whether:

* the original business case objectives were achieved
* agreed service levels are being met
* IT services are being managed effectively
* the volume of problems and change is acceptable
* security is effective
* users are satisfied with the service provided.

Although this review may be conducted by members of the original project team, it is recommended that a separate team is called on to provide a more objective view. On completion of the review, a report should be written which contains an assessment and recommendations for improvement. The report should be submitted to the IT Services Manager.

5.1.3 Ongoing management

Unlike other modules in the IT Infrastructure Library, Computer Installation and Acceptance is a project with a defined end point. Ongoing management is covered by all of the other books in the Library such as Computer Operations Management, Problem Management and Service Level Management. From the point of equipment

Section 5
Post-implementation and audit

handover, IT service management disciplines should be in place and effective. Guidance can be obtained from the detailed descriptions contained in the relevant IT Infrastructure Library modules. The primary objective of these disciplines is to ensure that a high quality, cost-effective service is provided to the satisfaction of users.

5.1.4 Further installations

Future equipment needs will largely be based on service demands and business priorities which should be identified through the Capacity Management process. Section 3 may be used as guidance for the planning of further installations.

5.2 Dependencies

The primary dependency is the implementation of the new equipment and software. Another dependency is the availability of suitably skilled people to conduct the reviews. The dependencies identified in section 3.2 should also be considered.

5.3 People

The training covered in section 3.3.9 should be supplemented by practical experience of using the new equipment and software. Keeping skills up-to-date, through formal classroom training and practical experience, is essential to keep abreast of a rapidly changing technical environment. Training should have been completed for staff involved in the post-implementation review, backup staff and users.

5.4 Timing

The recommended timing of reviews is as follows:

* a project evaluation review should be conducted as soon as possible after handover

* a post-implementation review should be undertaken six to twelve months after the commencement of live running.

The IT Infrastructure Library
Computer Installation and Acceptance

Section 6
Benefits, costs and possible problems

6. Benefits, costs and possible problems

6.1 Benefits

This module creates a framework for IT Services Management to plan efficiently for the successful implementation of new hardware and software.

The major benefit to be gained from following the rigorous project management approach advocated in this module is the reduction of the risk to the business which is inherent in any large complex project. Organizations which are dependent on their IT services are extremely vulnerable to disruption of those services. Specific benefits which can be expected from using the guidance in this module include:

* successful planning for and implementation of the new equipment and software
* minimal disruption of IT services both during and after installation
* meeting of timescales for acceptance trials
* fewer teething problems due to human error
* effective use of time by everyone involved in the planning, installation and acceptance trial phases
* more efficient IT services by having good service management processes in operation
* secure IT services
* improved staff productivity
* increased user satisfaction through the efficient introduction of new IT services.

6.2 Costs

Given that there are resources and costs associated with purchasing any new equipment and/or accommodation, any additional costs due to following the advice in this book should be minimal. Time and effort spent in planning and managing the project will be repaid by avoiding expensive mistakes and delays. Consideration should be given to the costs of not following the guidance in this module, which may be considerable if the installation and acceptance are not properly planned and co-ordinated.

The main costs of planning and implementation are likely to be:

* supporting the project team
* time to produce or amend procedures
* training of staff
* implementation of service management disciplines, if the computer centre is new.

6.3 Possible problems

It is likely that problems will occur during the project management cycle. The objective of IT Services Management and the project team should be to minimize them as far as possible through sound planning techniques. The use of a recognized project management methodology should allow problems to be detected and resolved before they can have a serious impact on the schedule. The most likely areas where problems will arise are:

* staff resistance to change
* poor project management
* late handover of accommodation, and delivery of equipment and software
* integration of hardware, software, networks, etc from different suppliers
* user expectations not satisfied.

6.3.1 Resistance to change

In most organizations, the need to replace or upgrade hardware and software will be seen as a logical progression to keep pace with increased service demands from customers. However, there may be some resistance to changes in working practices. This is not uncommon in the Operations area, where changes in technology and processes may be seen as reducing the traditional role and skills of operators. The overall effect is likely to be a lack of commitment, resulting in inefficiency, delay in responding to problems and procedural errors. These problems should not be underestimated and will need to be carefully handled by the IT Services Manager. Training and consultation with staff at every stage of the project will help to alleviate these problems.

Section 6
Benefits, costs and possible problems

6.3.2 Project Management

The most serious constraints to the success of the project are likely to be lack of good project management and availability of staff. This will result in the project running late and over budget. As a consequence there may be serious damage to the business or, at least, severe corporate or political embarrassment.

The single, most effective way of reducing this problem lies in the selection of the project manager (see section 3.3.3).

6.3.3 Accommodation handover and equipment delivery

Timely handover of computer accommodation and receipt of new equipment and software is critical to the success of the implementation phase of the project. Any delays will affect the installation schedule and provision of services. There will be a consequential impact on business operations, financial costs and on the user attitude to the new equipment and IT services. The project manager must keep in constant contact with the builders and suppliers, so that he or she is instantly aware of any potential delays. Of course this is not the only source of delay, further delays will be caused by the failure of any of the acceptance tests, for example. The Project Manager should build a contingency factor into the project plan to take this into account.

6.3.4 Integration of multi-vendor equipment

In addition to the difficulties of synchronizing the delivery and acceptance of equipment from different suppliers there is the technical difficulty of integrating hardware, software and communications equipment. This requires considerable expertise which, unless it is available from within the organization, should be bought in.

6.3.5 User expectations

The main problem likely to arise with the user community is that their expectations of the new equipment and services will not be satisfied (despite their involvement in specifying service levels). Contributing factors will include lack of awareness of new equipment and services, poor or variable response times and a lack of functionality, particularly from new software and applications. These will result in a lack of acceptance of the new services and a decline in morale. It is important to keep users fully aware of the progress of the project by means of publicity campaigns and ensure that all users receive appropriate training.

7. Tools

7.1 Introduction

In the context of this module, tools are primarily used by designers, planners and project teams responsible for computer installation and acceptance.

7.2 Types of tool

There are various, discrete tools which address individual areas of computer installation and acceptance, but overall they act in support of a project as a whole. The types of tool required cover the following areas:

* project management
* security risk analysis
* design
* configuration management (including cable management)
* spreadsheet
* word processing.

7.2.1 Project Management

The project should be supported by a management methodology, such as PRINCE, which addresses the various aspects of a project:

* organization
* plans
* controls
* end-products
* activities.

Each of these aspects is supported by documentation, including Gantt charts, activity schedules, PERT networks and dependency diagrams.

Many project management software tools are available; they range in cost from approximately £100 at the low end of the PC range, to over £500,000 for minicomputer and mainframe versions. Different packages have different strengths.

When deciding on which to use, the following points will need to be borne in mind:

* cost
* ease of use
* functionality
* quality of supporting documentation
* quality of output
* compatibility with other software.

A description of the various types of project management software is given in the 'A' set of IS Guides, especially **A Project Manager's Guide**. Typical packages include ARTEMIS (Metier), Project Manager's Workbench (Hoskyns), Super Project (Computer Associates) and Project for Windows (Microsoft Corp.).

7.2.2 Security risk analysis

The purpose of security risk analysis is to study the likelihood and level of impacts occurring which will affect the security of the installation. With the information gained, plans for managing the risk can be made. The CCTA Risk Analysis and Management Method (CRAMM) includes a tool to assist in this process.

CRAMM runs on an IBM PC or compatible machine.

7.2.3 Design and modelling

Design and modelling tools will already have been used in the building of computer accommodation; they are also essential to the planning and implementation of the computer room layout. Clear, scale drawings will need to be produced, both as an aid to design and for communicating clearly to contractors. The diagrams should include machine clearances, weights and dimensions, cable lengths and routeing. Models will also be needed to conduct 'what if' exercises as the design activity develops.

Computer-aided design (CAD) brings the drawing board to the computer. Its advantage over a manual approach lies in its greater productivity and accuracy and its ability to be linked to databases of information about items such as materials used and legislation.

CAD packages are available in mainframe and PC versions. Some specialised tools, such as Graphic Data Centre Manager (GDCM, from Hardware Planning Services) combine drawing capability with database facilities to enable planning and design of new computer accommodation, modify existing accommodation, maintain up-to-date drawings and keep an inventory of equipment.

7.2.4 Configuration Management

These tools incorporate a database containing a complete record of all the configuration items which make up an IT infrastructure and the relationships between them. It is an essential tool for Problem, Change and Configuration Managers. (It may be necessary to use a separate tool for some specialized applications such as cable management if the configuration management tool does not provide the required functionality).

Products which support Configuration Management include Assyst (Axios), CA/Netman (Computer Associates), INFO/MAN (IBM) and PCMS (SQL Software Ltd).

7.2.5 Spreadsheet

Among their many uses, spreadsheets are a valuable tool to the Project Manager, helping with project costing, budgeting, and the production of high quality graphical information for reporting to senior management. Most spreadsheet packages are available on PCs, examples are too numerous to mention.

7.2.6 Word Processing

Word processing tools are another important aid to the Project Manager in providing the efficient production of agendas, minutes, status reports and other documents of good quality and to a common standard.

The IT Infrastructure Library
Computer Installation and Acceptance

Section 8
Bibliography

8. Bibliography

An Overview of CRAMM. CCTA, London, 1990.

CCTA IS Guide A5: A Project Manager's Guide - ISBN 0 471 92525 X.

CCTA IS Guide B2: The Feasibility Study - ISBN 0 471 92527 6.

CCTA IS Guide B3: The Full Study - ISBN 0 471 92528 4.

CCTA IS Guide B5: The Operational Requirement - ISBN 0 471 92530 6.

CCTA IS Guide B6: Procurement - ISBN 0 471 92531 4.

CCTA IS Guide C4: Security and Privacy - ISBN 0 471 92537 3.

All of the above published by John Wiley and Sons Ltd, Chichester, 1989.

Computer Data Centre Design - A Guide for Planning, Designing, Constructing, and Operating Computer Data Centres. Robert F Halper. - ISBN 0 471 82579 4. John Wiley, New York, 1985.

Guide to procurement within the Total Acquisition Process, CCTA, 1991.

Health and Safety (Display Screen Equipment) Regulations, 1992. HMSO, London, 1992.

IBM General Information Manual, Installation Manual - Physical Planning (Ref, GC22-7072-2). IBM, New York, 1990.

IEE Regulations for Electrical Installations. Blackwell Scientific, Oxford, 1991.

Information Technology and Buildings - A Practical Guide for Designers. - ISBN 0 947 877 33 9. Butler Cox plc, London, 1989.

Planning the Corporate Data Centre. Butler Cox Foundation. Butler Cox plc, London, 1987.

PRINCE manuals comprising:

    Introduction to PRINCE

    PRINCE Management Guide

    PRINCE Technical Guide

    PRINCE Quality Guide

    PRINCE Configuration Management Guide

ISBN 1 85554 012 6. The set is published by National Computing Centre, Manchester, 1990.

SSADM and Capacity Planning. CCTA Information Systems Engineering Library. ISBN 0 11 330577 X. HMSO, London, 1992.

Annex A. Glossary of terms

Acronyms and abbreviations used in this module

BS	British Standard
CAD	Computer-aided Design
CCTA	The Government Centre for Information Systems
CCTV	Closed Circuit Television
CI	Configuration Item
CMDB	Configuration Management Database
CPU	Central Processing Unit
CRAMM	CCTA Risk Analysis and Management Method
IEE	Institute of Electrical Engineers
IS	Information System
ISE	Information Systems Engineering
ISO	International Standards Organization
IT	Information Technology
OR	Operational Requirement
PA	Public Address
PC	Personal Computer
PERT	Programme Evaluation and Review Technique
PRINCE	PRojects IN Controlled Environments
RFC	Request for Change
RFQ	Request for Quotation
SLA	Service Level Agreement
SSADM	Structured Systems Analysis and Design Method

Definitions used in this module

Accommodation Design Brief	A detailed specification of computer accommodation and environmental requirements.

The IT Infrastructure Library
Computer Installation and Acceptance

Configuration Item	A component of an IT infrastructure, normally the smallest item that can be changed independently of other components. Configuration Items may vary widely in complexity, size and type, from an entire system (including all hardware, software and documentation) to a single program module or minor hardware component.
Configuration Management	The process of identifying and defining the configuration items in a system, recording and reporting on their status, controlling changes to them and verifying their completeness and correctness.
Downtime	The amount of time that a service or system (whole or in part) is not available for use.
Fourth generation language	A high-level programming language, capable of producing prototype models of systems and applications both quickly and with a high degree of functionality. It could be used to generate a trial workload, in this context.
Greenfield site	New computer accommodation designed and built from the ground up.
IT Operations Bridge	The combination, in one physical location, of Computer Operations, Network Control and the Help Desk.
Minimum Trial System	The minimum combination of hardware and software which is defined in the contract as being necessary to process the specified workload during the acceptance trial.
Operational Requirement	A document forming a step in the procurement process, containing a complete statement of the procuring organization's requirements, addressed to any potential supplier of equipment or services, and designed to draw from each supplier a proposal describing in detail how the supplier could meet the requirements.
Request for Change	A form or screen, used to record details of a request for change to any component of an IT infrastructure or any aspect of IT services.
Request for Quotation	A request to potential suppliers to supply detailed specifications on relevant products.
Service Level Agreement	The written agreement or 'contract' between the users and the IT service provider which documents the agreed service levels for an IT service.
Termination frames	Hardware which provides termination circuitry for telecommunications networks.

Annex B. Acceptance procedures

This Annex provides an outline of the procedures for running acceptance trials under CCTA procurement procedures. Users of the CCTA Model Agreements should read this Annex in conjunction with the appropriate Schedules (see below) to the System Supply Agreement for more detailed information. Non-government readers are likely to find the main principles are generally applicable to their circumstances.

A Model Agreement consists of a set of contractual clauses together with a number of Schedules which describe, for instance, the goods and services to be supplied. The two Schedules which are relevant to the acceptance of computer systems are:

* Preparation for and performance of acceptance procedures
* Acceptance procedures and acceptance criteria.

A further Schedule which describes the system to be supplied, also contains a description of what is to be considered as the Minimum Trial System (see below).

The Model Agreements are not intended to be regarded as a standard or immutable set of terms and conditions. Each project and customer has specific needs and the Model Agreement requires tailoring to meet those needs. Model Agreements contain clauses which are specifically necessary for public sector contracts and are not suitable for use in the private sector in their present form.

Note that throughout these Model Agreements, the term **Authority** is used to denote the organization placing a contract with a **Contractor** (the provider of goods or services).

B.1 Preparation for and performance of acceptance procedures

This Schedule sets out the activities and responsibilities of the two parties in relation to preparation for acceptance procedures and performance of acceptance procedures. It also contains the terms and conditions describing what constitutes downtime (and what is excluded), how to calculate serviceability, and what constitutes the trial workload.

B.1.1 Preparation for acceptance procedures

Preparation activities and responsibilities are as follows.

Appoint representatives
Both parties appoint a representative at least a month before the start of the Acceptance Procedures Period. This is the period, specified in another Schedule - the Implementation Plan, within which the acceptance procedures must be performed. The Acceptance Procedures Period must allow for restarts and repeats within the contractual maximum of three times the nominal Workload Trials Period (see B3.1).

Agree format
At least two weeks before the start of the Acceptance Procedures Period the representatives agree the format of the incident reports (see B.1.4). These are the reports which are used to record any incident or to log any question arising from an unusual event. A contractual incident report is only deemed to have been resolved when it has been signed off by the Authority's representative.

Certify readiness
The Contractor must certify in writing that the system is ready to undergo the acceptance procedure.

Identification list
The Contractor must supply a list of the delivered system showing the serial number of each item (or other means of identification). This list is to be kept updated by the Contractor throughout the Acceptance Procedures Period.

Any other preparations for acceptance procedures which are agreed should be detailed in this part of the Schedule.

B.1.2 Performance of acceptance procedures

This part of the Schedule consists mainly of the Authority's responsibilities during the Acceptance Procedures Period, such as:

* providing media and consumables required for the acceptance procedures

* maintaining records of metered time, elapsed time and operating time for each unit, also records of the environmental conditions

* providing the necessary operating staff - these must be listed in the Schedule which describes the Authority's Responsibilities.

Annex B
Acceptance procedures

Any other acceptance procedures to be performed by either party should be detailed in this section of the Schedule.

B.1.3 Downtime

Downtime is measured at two levels: at the unit of hardware and at the overall Minimum Trial System. This part of the Schedule sets out the conditions which govern whether or not an Incident is admissible as downtime. Further information may be obtained by reading the Model Agreement.

B.1.4 Calculation of serviceability

Serviceability is calculated as follows:

$$\frac{\text{Operational Use Time}}{\text{Operational Use Time} + \text{Downtime}} \times 100$$

Where:

Operational Use Time is the accumulated time during which the Minimum Trial System or a unit is operating correctly and available for use (minimum of 100 hours)

Downtime is the period when the Minimum Trial System or a unit is not available to process the workload.

This means that a daily log must be kept which records:

* the time when the trial commences and ends
* brief details of each incident that occurs.

For each incident the following minimum information should be recorded on an Incident Report:

* whether or not the incident was contractual (ie a fault or failure of the system under test)
* the time when the Contractor was notified that an incident has occurred
* the time when the system or unit was handed back by the Contractor
* the unit or units affected by an incident
* the reason for the incident
* the action taken by the Contractor or the Authority to restore the unit or system for use.

B.2 Acceptance procedures and acceptance criteria

This Schedule describes the conditions for acceptance, and the acceptance procedures to be applied together with the corresponding acceptance criteria. The acceptance procedures are split into three activities:

* inspection
* functionality tests
* workload trial.

B.2.1 Conditions for acceptance

The conditions for acceptance state that tests under the three categories shall be recorded as successful if the relevant acceptance criteria have been met within the Acceptance Procedures Period.

If the workload trial has been successful in respect of the Minimum Trial System, but one or more units of hardware have not achieved the required serviceability, the system should be accepted subject to the repair or replacement of the defective units.

If there are any unresolved Incident Reports at the end of the Acceptance Procedures Period, the procedures should be recorded as unsuccessful.

If, at the end of the Acceptance Procedures Period, the acceptance has been recorded as successful, the Authority must confirm to the Contractor, in writing, that the system is accepted. The Configuration Manager should be informed of this acceptance and the status of the configuration items updated accordingly.

B.2.2 Acceptance procedures

Acceptance procedures must be specified in the Schedule for each of the three activities.

B.2.2.1 Inspection

Inspection consists of ensuring that all hardware (and features) are present and in accordance with the contract, and identifying any cosmetic defects. Checks must be made to ensure that correct versions of software are installed and that documentation is complete (including the correct number of copies). As this activity can be conducted in parallel with the formal trial there is no need to allow separate time for it. However it should not be neglected as any deficiencies or inconsistencies are best dealt with before acceptance is complete.

B.2.2.2 Functionality tests

Functionality tests are the procedures that demonstrate the performance and functionality of the hardware and software being supplied. These tests are run to check the functionality specified in the OR. Whilst the means of conducting many of these functionality tests may be readily available from the Contractor's own sources, some effort may be required to devise tests which are specifically designed to establish that requirements have been met.

Functionality tests should be agreed during the contractual negotiations (the supplier needs to be aware of them in formulating his bid). A schedule must be agreed detailing the precise requirements of content, criteria and duration of demonstrations.

It is strongly recommended that the workload trial does not commence until functionality tests (with minor exceptions) have been completed satisfactorily.

B.2.2.3 Workload trial

The workload trial consists of running a specified and agreed 'normal live workload', within the agreed hours of service cover over the 'Workload Trials Period' ie a specified period (20 days suggested, depending on complexity).

As an example, this workload may consist of 70% productive work supplemented by 30% simulated work to bring the system utilisation up to that which is the eventual intention of the organization. Provided that both parties can agree, other variations of workload may be used. Over the Workload Trials Period the 'Minimum Trial System', which should be agreed and specified in the Agreement, is required to achieve a serviceability level which is specified in this Schedule. For example, 97% for the minimum system, with individual units achieving 92% or 96% as appropriate.

Acceptance

All functionality tests must be completed within the Acceptance Procedures Period. There is no constraint on the number of attempts the Contractor may have within this

The IT Infrastructure Library
Computer Installation and Acceptance

period. In addition, the serviceability must meet the criteria specified both for the Minimum Trial System and for individual units within a maximum of three times the specified period. Within this, the criteria must be met over a contiguous period of specified duration (apart from any suspension that may have been agreed due to circumstances beyond the Contractor's control). So, for instance, in the case of a 20-day specified Workload Trials Period, the serviceability would be calculated at the end of the 20th day. If the criteria had not been met then the period would continue for another day. At the end of the 21st day serviceability would be calculated for days 2-21. This process can continue for days 3-22, 4-23, etc until the criteria are met or 60 days have expired. (For the consequence in the latter case see 'Failure' below).

If there is any doubt about the success of the trial, the Authority should seek appropriate contractual advice. In circumstances where the principal criteria are met, but some minor problems are outstanding, the organization may wish to accept the system and agree that certain sums of money will be retained pending resolution of the identified discrepancies. Such grounds could be that a non-critical unit had failed to meet its serviceability criterion (in which case acceptance of that unit would be deferred until the criterion had been met), an incomplete minor demonstration, a minor software fault, cosmetic defect or insufficient copies of documentation. The real test is whether the organization feels that it can process its future scheduled workload with the continuing presence of the deficiency.

Failure

Failure to sign off the acceptance procedures is not an option that an organization is going to pursue lightly. However, it needs to be stressed that the Contractor has the opportunity to remedy the Breach of Contract position in which he will be placed as a result of failure and that termination of contract is the last resort. Should such circumstances arise it is recommended that government organizations should seek the urgent advice and support of CCTA. In cases of doubt it is better, in the longer term, to invoke the terms of the contract than to avoid conflict and hope that "it will work out all right in the end".

Annex B
Acceptance procedures

The circumstances of failure are:

- major demonstration not completed within the Acceptance Procedures Period

or

- serviceability criterion for Minimum Trial System (or minimum subsystem) not met in 3 x specified period.

    (In the example quoted above, if day 60 had been reached without meeting the criterion - i.e. days 41-60 had been unsuccessful)

or

- outstanding incident reports

    (When an incident has occurred, which has not been resolved to the satisfaction of the Authority by the completion of the Acceptance Procedures Period, then the trial should be recorded as unsuccessful. Such incidents may be a 'last day' failure which means that the system is actually unserviceable at the end of the Trial Period or, the more problematic, one-off software interaction fault. Whether or not to recommend failure (see B.2.2.3) will depend upon the severity of the problem and its likely impact on live work. It is recommended that the Authority seeks contractual advice before making such recommendation and that no intimations are communicated to the Contractor until that advice has been considered).

Annex C. Procurement guidance

This Annex supplements the detail contained in section 3.1.2.1. The content is more likely to be of interest to non-government organizations since, in general, their procurement processes are different from those used by government departments.

Planning for the ordering of new equipment and software should be developed between the IT Services organization and Procurement. The sequence of activities will generally be as follows:

* define the equipment needed
* develop equipment specifications
* identify a list of potential suppliers
* develop and issue a Request for Quotation (RFQ)
* receive responses to the RFQs
* review quotations
* select suppliers
* order equipment
* receive equipment
* install, test and hand over equipment.

For each piece of equipment to be ordered, there should be a statement of requirement, covering:

* purpose
* function
* performance and capacity projections
* relationship with other equipment.

The system and device configurations must be specified to identify clearly the items to be ordered. A detailed specification should be produced and issued, through Procurement, to potential suppliers and quotations requested. The issued RFQ should contain:

* equipment description
* delivery date
* installation date

* supporting documentation
* maintenance requirements
* spare parts
* consumables
* training needs.

The supplier's reply should be accompanied by bid quotations which respond to the RFQ.

Some organizations have formal procedures for reviewing bid quotations, which act as protection against accusations of unfair practices. All bids relating to a particular contract should be opened for review at the same time. Selection of a supplier should be based on a fair analysis of the quotations submitted. When a supplier has been selected, an order should be developed and submitted by Procurement.

Procurement should follow up the progress of each item ordered, keeping in regular contact with IT Services or the project team responsible for the installation. As the equipment arrives, it should be inspected, installed and tested. There should be a Configuration Management database record for each item ordered.

Annex D. Standards

D.1 Introduction

This annex provides guidance on British Standards and regulations for computer accommodation designers. The design and installation must take into consideration local and government regulations, to ensure that all requirements are met. In the case of conflict, the most stringent criteria should apply.

D.2 Computer room sizes

The following room dimensions are intended as guidance to designers and will give an idea of the generally accepted sizes. The actual size of the room will obviously depend on the amount of equipment to be installed. The Accommodation Design Brief will specify the accommodation requirements.

Large
: 500 metres square to 2,500 metres square, accommodating multiple large central processors with controllers and storage devices.

Medium
: 250 metres square to 500 metres square, accommodating one or two large central processors with controllers and storage devices or multiple medium-sized processors, controllers and storage devices.

Small
: 50 metres square to 250 metres square, accommodating single medium-sized processors and storage devices or multiple small processors, controllers and storage devices.

D.3 Electrical and mechanical design standards

D.3.1 General

The design and installation of electrical and mechanical systems must be safe, energy efficient, emphasize simplicity of layout and use components which comply with the relevant standards.

D.3.2 Safety

Safety standards must ensure protection against personal injury and property damage and comply with the current edition of the following:

* Chartered Institution of Building Services Engineers guide to current practice

- IEE Regulations for Electrical Installations
- Electrical Supply regulations
- Electricity at Work regulations
- Health and Safety (Display Screen Equipment) regulations
- Health and Safety at Work etc. Act.

D.3.3 Equipment

Manufactured equipment must include the necessary certification to demonstrate compliance to IEE regulations and the EC directive on electromagnetic compatibility.

D.3.4 Installation

The installation should comply with British Standards and meet the requirements of the:

- Health and Safety Executive
- Building Control Officer
- Fire Officer
- Insurers.

D.4 Fire protection and life safety systems

D.4.1 General

The design and installation of fire protection and life safety systems must provide optimum protection against personal injury, property damage and business interruption.

D.4.2 Safety

The design, equipment approval and installation should conform to the current edition of the following British Standards:

- BS5839 - Fire detection and alarm systems in buildings
- BS6266 - Code of practice for "Fire Protection for electronic data processing installations"
- BS5306 - Fire extinguishing systems installation and equipment in premises

Annex D
Standards

- * BS5588 - Fire precautions in the design and construction of buildings
- * BS5499 - Fire safety signs, notices and graphic symbols
- * BS6259 and BS5428 - Public address, planning, installation and components.

Annex E. Installation procedures

This Annex supplements section 3.1.2.6 and forms a checklist for defining installation procedures.

E.1 Hardware

The following topics will be of relevance when planning for the arrival of hardware:

* computer room ready with all services having been tested and signed off
* all physical security and health and safety arrangements in place
* road access to the building (Have the local police been contacted? Are there likely to be traffic difficulties?)
* hire of plant, eg cranes, moving equipment
* electrical and mechanical services available
* all equipment cabling either available or known to be arriving in time for the hardware installation
* timely arrival of the hardware (This will need to be carefully co-ordinated if more than one supplier is involved. Procurement have a key role to play in this activity)
* availability of associated documentation for the hardware, including installation instructions
* availability of the supplier's engineers to support the installation
* successful power-on of all hardware units and tests of the emergency power-off circuits
* labelling and recording of all new equipment, through the Configuration Management system (If there is a large amount of equipment being installed, a bar coding system may be considered)
* training of operations and support staff in the use of computer room facilities and emergency shut-down procedures
* operational procedures available
* the scheduling of any associated equipment relocation.

E.2 System and applications software

The arrival of system software and application packages should be synchronized with the delivery of hardware and include checking that:

* the arrival of all software and associated documentation was as ordered
* the support of supplier staff is available if required
* a test plan, including evaluation criteria for successful completion, is defined
* movement of any existing software and application data files is scheduled
* training plans are in place for operations staff in the:
    - system operating procedures
    - security procedures
    - recovery procedures
* a record of all new software and applications is included in the Configuration Management database.

Further information is contained in the IT Infrastructure Library module on **Testing an IT Service for Operational Use**.

IT Infrastructure Library
Computer Installation and Acceptance

Comments Sheet

CCTA hopes that you find this book both useful and interesting. We will welcome your comments and suggestions for improving it.
Please use this form or a photocopy, and continue on a further sheet if needed.

From:

        Name

        Organization

        Address

        Telephone

COVERAGE
Does the material cover your needs?
If not, then what additional material would you like included.

CLARITY
Are there any points which are unclear?
If yes, please detail where and why.

ACCURACY
Please give details of any inaccuracies found.

If more space is required for these or other comments, please continue overleaf.

IT Infrastructure Library
Computer Installation and Acceptance

Comments Sheet

OTHER COMMENTS

Return to: IT Infrastructure Management Services
             CCTA,
             Gildengate House
             Upper Green Lane
             NORWICH, NR3 1DW

Further information

Further information on the contents of this module can be obtained from:

IT Infrastructure Management Services
CCTA
Gildengate House
Upper Green Lane
NORWICH
NR3 1DW.

Telephone: 0603 694855
(GTN: 3014 4855)